BREATHING PURE AIR

TRUE CLIMBING STORIES BY:

GARY A METTERNICH

ABOUT THE AUTHOR

The author grew up in the Medford area of Southern Oregon and lived there until joining the Marine Corps. He didn't start climbing until thirty-four years of age. What drew him to the mountains? It was the serene beauty, peace, and excitement of God's nature. Even though beginning his climbing at that age, he has managed to make over 220 major summits, mostly in the Northwestern United States, but others in Canada, Mexico and South America.

Today, he resides in Redmond, Oregon, an area of unbelievable beauty of lakes, rivers, streams and mountains. He still climbs mountains (easier ones), hikes, boats, fishes, snowboards and tries to spend as much time outdoors as possible.

He believes that God's Nature is a gift to all people, and his plan was to have it available to all. In Nature our spirit is healed.

This book is written for people never having the opportunity to experience the nature of the outdoors, or just a taste of it. Also, it is for those outdoor enthusiasts that would like to know what it is like to fulfill an adventurous climb. This book contains short true stories of **thrill, pain, camaraderie, nature's beauty and completeness.** It is also stories of true survival **MIRACLES.**

INDEX

INDEX PAGE 2

PREFACE

Over the years, the question has often been asked, "Why do you climb mountains?" Sometimes it is followed by another question, "Because its' there?" Of course my answer has never been "Because its' there!" That was an answer made famous by George Mallory, a legend in the climbing world, and probably because he had gotten tired of answering the same old question time and time again. In fact, it was a logical answer, because the question is truly a difficult one to thoroughly answer.

I am writing this book as a reflection on some of the great experiences that I was involved in over a period of twenty-five plus years. These events have been firmly implanted in my mind, and the years have not diminished them. In these stories, I will try to answer the question of why I climb mountains. I will try to cover the five main reasons why I spent so much time leaving the comfort of a warm and safe home to venture into a beautiful, but sometimes hostile environment, requiring the ultimate in physical and mental exertion. These reasons will include, *for the thrill of it, the beauty of nature, camaraderie, physical and mental challenges,* and finally, *the spiritual aspect.* To those mountaineers whose only goals are to see how many mountains they can climb, commonly referred to as "peak baggers," and to other outdoor enthusiasts that are literally hooked on their own adrenaline, striving only to break records, this book will seem boring. The reasons I give may be too lofty, or if you will, overly romantic. These stories certainly are not intended for those. My stories are for those that love the outdoors, and have had a taste of what it can offer, or maybe just a desire to experience more of it.

The challenges offered in climbing, as well as other life obstacles are simply defined in a poem, written in the early seventies that I had hanging in my office along with a drawing of a climber climbing steep ice. It was written by an airline pilot and one of America's promising young climbers, whom after writing this poem died in the Pamir Range of Russia. His name is Jon Gary Ulin, and the poem follows:

TO SEEK THE HEIGHTS

**To be at his best, man must climb the unknown, this is his quest.
Whether his mountain is granite and ice,
The nature of things, or the problems of life, His character gains.
He challenges his mind, body and soul
And the point of it all, is to achieve a goal.
Security and comfort are part of the price, but in the balance is a genuine life.**

There is another wonderful definition of climbing that came from the diary of Hermann Buhl, a famous German climber who in the early fifties was in the race to be the first on the summit of Mt. Everest, the world's tallest mountain. This definition touches deeply my reasons for climbing. Like Gary Ulin, Hermann Buhl also died on a mountain, doing the thing that he loved most. He died on Nanga Parbat in 1953, another eight thousand meter peak in the Himalayas, the same year that Mt. Everest was finally summited. This vivid description in his diary goes like this:

It is there that I am most alive. To climb on a clear blue day, the sun shimmering off the Ice, the wind biting into my soul, that is where I am at peace with myself; completely alone, and yet in unison with the mountains, with nature, with God. Other men may talk of such things, but only a climber can truly know that. When one has climbed a great mountain and stands on its peak, it is then that one realizes it is not a mountain that one has conquered, but ourselves.

There are no words to describe the unforgettable impressions of such a moment. There are pictures that obliterate mere human happenings; shining visions which seals ones heart, wiping out all memories of sorrow and disappointment.

I also wrote this book, to explain to my children, friends and clients why I was absent so often from home, office and social functions. I know that to many of my acquaintances I may have seemed a bit insane, sometimes risking a lot for that special time in the mountains, especially when they saw a worn out, weather- beaten person that looked like he had just fought in a great battle. Has it been worth it? Absolutely! I still have dreams of climbing, and try to get into the wilderness as often as possible. The climbs of today are easier and less risky, but still fully satisfying. I will always cherish those times of peace, beauty and friendship experienced over the years.

Gary Metternich

CHAPTER I

BUMPS AND BRUISES

How does one really know the exact time that they first started climbing? Was it an attempt to get on top of the chair, or possibly was it trying to get over the rails protecting you inside the baby crib? From the time that we begin to crawl, climbing becomes a natural part of our movements. We really can't remember these first experiences, because we are too young at the time. However, we can remember how we failed to achieve the climb and fell flat on our face. Many of these first experiences of failure, and the resulting pain, are planted indelibly in our memories.

I was no exception. I probably had my share of falling off formidable objects, bumping my nose, bruising body parts, and then crying for Mom. As I grew older, and not having acquired a total fear from my failures, the goals became larger, and more daring.

The first experience that I can remember that had all the elements of climbing something difficult; curiosity, flow of adrenaline, joy, fear, stark terror, and then terrible pain, was when I was between two and three years old. My family had taken a vacation to the California coast at Smith River. For some reason, my mother took only me down to the beach for a picnic, leaving my brothers with my dad. There was a large rocky area amidst the sand and near the ocean water, but safe from the incoming waves, and sheltered from the wind. It was a warm sunny day, and my mother spread out a picnic cloth, and then began to relax with her feet in the warm sand while reading a book. She probably was thinking that she really did not have to pay much attention to me, since children my age can spend hours being satisfied just digging into the sand with sticks or rocks. The worse that usually happens to a child is that they end up eventually putting a handful of the sand in their mouth, hoping that it tastes good like apple pie.

As my mother relaxed and sunned herself, I glanced around at the strange looking rocks that formed a semi-circle nearly around us, beginning at the water's edge. We certainly didn't have anything like this at home, with mainly trees, shrubs and grass as our playground. As I faced the ocean, slightly to my left was a nice rounded large rock, with lots of rough edges and little pockets, some of which still had water in them from the high tide earlier. This rock looked giant to me, but it probably wasn't more than fifteen feet high. I'm sure that my mother was watching my every move, but probably thought there was no harm in letting me roam a little ways over to the rock since the tide was out, and there would be no danger of being swept away.

As I came closer to the rock, I could see convenient step-like indentations that I placed my feet on, and soon I had scampered up to the base of the steeper rock. I looked up, touched the rock with my hands, and was pleasantly surprised to find that the rock was rough, and had little cup-like features that made it easy to grasp. Soon, I was carefully going up the rock, trying to be careful that I did not fall over backwards, since the base below me was solid rock. Even at my young age, I suspected that any fall could hurt very much. My mother was either very interested in the book she was reading, or she wasn't worried that I would climb much higher and hurt myself. At this point, I was confident. My heart was beating fast from the excitement, and I now had the feeling that possibly I could reach the top and actually look over at some spectacular view. I was more than half way up the rock and soon would be looking over the top of it, when I grabbed what looked like a good handhold in order to pull myself up to a point where my little foot could be planted firmly. All of a sudden, the rock that I had grabbed came out into my hand, causing me to lose my balance and to topple over backwards.

The next thing I remember was hitting the rock base below me, flat on my back! Upon impact, my head flew back and smacked the rough rock, almost knocking me unconscious. The pain was unbelievable! The rock that I landed on was not smooth, but had little ridges and knobs, and the result was pain throughout my whole back. Even worse, was the contact of my head on the rock. At first I saw stars, then my head was enveloped with throbbing pain. It hurt so bad that I could not even cry out to my mother. I just lay there whimpering. Quickly, she got up and came to my rescue. She probably thought I had suffered some serious injury, but other than suffering a headache, and some nice bruises on my head and back, I survived.

Since there were no rocks or hills to climb near where we lived, as I grew older I climbed anything that was available. Every oak and pine tree in our yard was scarred from the many climbs up them. There was an oak tree next to the carport with a protruding limb that offered a means of pulling myself up onto the roof. One day, I pulled myself onto the roof, and began running across the wooden shingles to gain the main roof of the house. It was after a recent rainstorm, and the shingles were as slick as ice. I slipped off, falling onto the chrome front bumper of the family auto. I landed on my back, causing a large gash in my back, but fortunately no broken bones.

My neighbors had many fruit trees. Often we would climb these trees, picking off the choice fruits. One day I climbed a beautiful, large cherry tree. Shimmying out along a large limb, I tried to reach out and pick that one beautiful cherry. The bark of the limb was slick, and I slipped off, falling ten feet to the concrete platform below. This time I broke my left wrist.

There was a mountain in our area that had the name John's Peak. It wasn't a real mountain, but a peak in the midst of a large forested area. It was quite a hike from our home, of a few miles. First up a long dirt road, then through brush, up a dry creek bed, then up steep loose sandy slopes to the summit. The main obstacle in this climb was that it was covered in areas with poison oak. I happened to be very allergic to poison oak, usually getting it two or three times a year. When I did get it, it would last several weeks, and my eyes would usually swell shut, with my face horribly deformed with scabs. All I had to do was to pet an animal that had it on its fur, and I would soon break out with it. It made my life miserable, but the call of the wild was stronger than my fear of the itchy rash, and so I ventured out, knowing what I had in store for myself. Backpacks and small climbing stoves in those days were not available to everyone, so I had to improvise as much as possible. This meant putting the drinking water in a gallon glass jug, grabbing a hatchet and matches, a few cans of pork and beans, a blanket off the bed and then throwing everything into a gunny sack for hauling. I attempted carrying the provisions with the sack thrown over my shoulder, but when heading up the steep loose slopes, I had to drag it behind me. On one occasion the water jug broke before reaching the summit, and my companions and I went without water until reaching home the next day.

I pursued these adventures, always with the goal of reaching the top of a peak and camping overnight below the beauty of the stars. Usually my companions and I spent a night in stark terror, listening to a mountain lion screaming in the distance, or the rustling of the bushes around us caused by the smaller critters out searching for food at night. The hot morning sun would wake us the next day exhausted from a miserable night's sleep, and sometimes half dying of thirst.

There was an ice cream cone shaped rock just a short way from the top of the peak, stuck vertically in the steep sandy slope. It was probably twenty feet high from the very bottom to the top. We found a small tree that had been blown over by the wind, still having enough limbs on it to grasp onto.

I would lean the tree from the steep slope, resting it on the top of the rock, and then climb up the tree. Once at the top, I liked to jump off the rock, approximately ten or twelve feet to the nearest loose, soft slope. It was imposing to be on the small top of the rock, especially looking down the outer side that was more than twenty feet down the slope. On one occasion, I took a friend named Fred hiking to the summit. On the way down I suggested that we climb this rock. He responded that he was not sure that he wanted to. I told him that it was real easy, and proceeded up the tree to the top. He gingerly followed to the top, and then I suggested jumping off. He certainly did not want to do that! I said that it was simple, and jumped off to show him. I waited, but he still did not want to. I then took the tree away from the rock and told him that he had to! After half an hour of persuasion, he finally jumped. He sprained both ankles! I barely got him home. His parents were so angry that they forbade me to ever come to their house again. Interestingly, years later I joined the Marines, and he followed suit a year or two later.

****

I was born in southern Oregon, just after the Great Depression. Both grandfathers were of German descent, with Gustav Ehlers, my grandfather on my mother's side being an immigrant from Germany. He had served in Kaiser Wilhelm's Prussian (German) army, but disliking the direction that he saw Germany heading towards, he left Germany and came to the United States on a tramp steamer as a cabin boy, landing in San Francisco. Later he moved to the Northwest, settling in Portland, Oregon.

Gustav was strong willed, and had a lean, strong frame of a body. He lost his wife to Scarlet Fever shortly after the third daughter was born. He never remarried, but raised the girls in a totalitarian household. A successful manager of a varnish manufacturing company, he lived to be ninety-four years old. Besides loving music (symphonic and opera) and reading, he was quite active physically. He jogged into his eighties, until he was forced to convert to walking five to ten miles daily. He had his own form of Isometrics which he did daily, keeping his body tight and in good condition. He was my favorite relative, and when he died at the age of ninety-four, I felt that I had lost a good friend. He was one person that I really looked up to and wanted to be like. The last time I had a good talk with him, he told me that he hated being old. He said his mind was as young as ever, but he could not read because of his cataracts, and was losing his hearing. He was deprived of doing the two things he loved most, his music and reading. One day he took off his shirt and showed me his muscular build which he was quite proud of. He died a couple of years later in his sleep.

My mother moved from Portland, Oregon to southern Oregon. As a young girl she had gone there to visit an aunt and uncle who owned a turkey ranch. She was just a year or two out of high school, and probably was tired of her father's strictness. It was there that she met my Dad, a handsome but wild lad who swept her off her feet. It was a different life style for this young lady from a proper city family. My Dad was a welder working in the logging industry, doing repair work on logging trucks. Loggers in those days were hellions who loved to drink and fight. My Dad was one of them, and according to his friends was one of the best wrestlers in the valley.

I was born the third child in the family. The second child died shortly after being born, so I became the second oldest of four boys. Times were extremely difficult in the years prior to the 2nd World War, and still not easy during the war years. Most people just had enough to get along on, with no extras. Housewives had to stretch the food budget, picking and canning many varieties of fruits and vegetables to feed a family. During the war it became even harder with the rationing of food, household supplies, gasoline and many other items that we now take for granted. The men spent many hours working at their jobs, six and sometimes seven days a week and twelve hours a day. Because of the shortage of men, women took jobs in the factories doing everything from making clothes to welding war equipment, and riveting airplanes together. The war changed the way Americans lived forever.

Even though it was during a difficult time in U.S. history, it was a good time to be young and growing up. Like most families, our family did not have much, but since we never knew what it was like to have a lot, we never missed things. As children, toys were almost non-existent. We learned to use our imagination a lot, spending our time outdoors playing cowboys and Indians, or games such as tag, and kick the can. Most of our toys were handmade, since either they were not available, or we could never afford them. We did have freedom that kids growing up today don't have. We could wander around and away from our home without worrying about someone abducting us. Crime was very rare where we lived, so we never feared anyone breaking into our house, or auto. Gangs were things that we only saw in the movies about New York or Chicago. Our house doors were never locked and you could always find the car keys in the ignition of the car. As a child, my security blanket was the family, and we always felt that we would be loved and well taken care of.

My Dad was the breadwinner in the family. He was rarely home it seemed, not only working the necessary long hours supporting a wife and four boys, but also spending much of his free time drinking and partying with the fellow employees and the good old boys who hung out near the shops where he worked. Because of his absence, my mother had most of the responsibility of raising four boys. Even though she was a slender woman with delicate features, she had a strong body, spending as many hours working in the home as my Dad outside it. Besides the cooking and house cleaning, she made sure the family had plenty to eat by picking fresh fruit and vegetables, and canning them. It seemed that anything that grew, she canned.

Even though Mom was reserved, behind her loving and responsible demeanor was a source of energy that longed to be tested. It was not until I was in my teens that I learned that she had had a strong desire for climbing. In the late 1920s when she was seventeen, she climbed Mt. Hood, the highest mountain in Oregon, with the Mazama Climbing Club of Portland, Oregon. In those days, they began the climb at Government Camp, located six to eight miles lower than the present lodge where most climbs begin. It was a two day climb, with the group spending one night camped out on the lower slopes of the mountain. In those days, ladies climbed with dresses, and all climbers used the alpine stock rather than an ice axe. In addition to this feat, a couple of years later, she and a girlfriend attempted soloing Mt. Rainier, a very formidable feat for even experienced mountaineers, and became stranded high on the mountain and had to be rescued. Maybe it was because of these inner desires and her high energy level, that as a mother she was a little more tolerant than normal with her four sons and their ensuing escapades.

As she no doubt had inherited her strength and the adventure-some spirit from her father, Gustav, I believe that my energy, and the resulting desire to be tested were inherited by me from my mother.

Growing up in the fifties was a wonderful time to be alive. It was an exciting time. After the World War was over, our country experienced tremendous industrial as well as social growth. Since not all our resources were going toward the war effort, people had more time to expand their personal lives. Entertainment was an integral part of our society, and we had our share of big name personalities, and our heroes.

11

During the war our famous individuals were Roosevelt, Churchill, Ike, Patton and others. And then in the fifties, we had names like Einstein, Marilyn and Elvis. In sports we had heroes such as DiMaggio and Mantle in baseball, and Roger Bannister who ran the first sub four-minute mile. We also had daring individuals exploring the world and space. Chuck Yeager broke the sound barrier in a Bell rocket plane. And then, there was the race to climb the highest mountain in the world, Everest. The first eight thousand meter peak, Annapurna, set the stage for the race, being climbed in 1950 by Maurice Herzog and his team. His team succeeded, but the price they paid physically was alarming. Now that an eight thousand meter peak had been climbed, the other tallest mountains were to be conquered. Everest, the highest in the world was on everyone's mind. Who would be the first to climb the highest mountain at the altitude of 29,009 ft.? It was a race between the British, Swiss and Germans. I watched the news reels at the theaters and read the articles in the papers. Seeing pictures of these marvelous men, with their goggles, bulky clothing, climbing gear, and the appearance of exhaustion and frostbite inspired me. In 1953 a team from New Zealand, including a Sherpa, finally conquered Everest. Sir Edmund Hillary, and Sherpa Tenzing Norgay were the first to stand on the highest point on earth.

.

With Everest climbed, man knew that he could survive at extreme high altitudes, even though highly dangerous, and it opened a race for the other giant mountains of the world. Little did I know what an impact these stories would have on me years later.

Organized sports and girls inhibited my outdoor activities during my teens, although I did jump at every chance to go fishing that came along. An elderly family friend named Gordon would call me now and then asking me to go fishing. I always dropped anything that I had scheduled and went. Sometimes we fished streams and rivers. When we did, I took off along the shore, exploring the rocks and beautiful pools of water, losing track of time, and then finding myself miles from our camp. I usually returned late, tired and hungry. God's nature seemed to pull me like a magnet.

****

After high school, I followed by boyhood dream of joining the Marine Corps. A friend of our family was a career Marine, having served in the Boxer Rebellion in China, the First World War, and Nicaragua, then as an instructor during the World War II. I was very impressed with him as a man. I listened to the stories and saw the movies of the Marines fighting in the Pacific during the war and decided that I also wanted to be a "Leatherneck."

I loved the training, especially the physical challenges such as forced marches with full battle gear. During our combat infantry training we averaged ten to twenty miles per day, up and down hills with names such as Old Smokey, and Big and Little Agony. These marches were more like runs, with the men in the rear of the platoons usually sprinting to keep up with the others. Our leaders sometimes pushed us to the point where men were actually passing out from exhaustion. I liked these challenges, both physical and mental, feeling that I was part of something special. I had never been challenged like this before, and it was here that I learned that the mind was stronger than the body. Sometimes your body told you that it could go no further, and the mind would respond, *you must*! *You have no choice, but have to gut it out*! Little did I know that someday this conditioning of the body and mind would help me face a few severe trials in the mountains.

After nearly four years of military service, I decided that it was time to go back to civilian life and resume my education. I was filled with sadness at leaving the Corps. It had transformed me from a soft teenager to a disciplined man, making me more capable of growing in other aspects of life. I knew that any further growth in the Marines would be slow, and, if I ever wanted to marry and settle down, the Marine Corps was not the place to be burdened down by a family. Living out of a sea bag, and always on twenty-four hours' notice to be able to move out, did not make a stable husband. I was honorably discharged in January 1959 and went home to Portland, Oregon where I had lived just prior to enlisting.

The next few years were what you might call *party time*. After getting a decent paying job at a paint manufacturing company, I promptly set out to do the things that I had been deprived of for so long: namely cars, partying and women. Somehow, during this stretch of a few years of active social life I was able to get some education. I even made the decision that I would major in accounting, and try to become a professional, a Certified Public Accountant. After experiencing three years working in unhealthy conditions at the factory, I knew that I did not want to do it any longer.

I had not accomplished much in three years, but it was a nice change from the regimented life of the military. It was truly the first time in my life that I was free. About the time that I became tired of the party scene, I met a wholesome girl with a totally different life style. Her name was Carol, and she helped me to settle down and work towards my professional goal. We were married a year later, and soon after moved to the small eastern Oregon town of La Grande, where I took a job as a bottom level accountant in a CPA firm. My plan was to continue studying and at the same time gain the necessary experience to qualify me for the CPA exam. The following autumn, we had our first child, a daughter that we named Teresa.

Working hard, studying, and being a father proved to be exhausting, and it robbed me of most of my free time. Eastern Oregon is a beautiful place to live if you are involved in outdoor activities such as hunting, fishing, hiking or raising animals. I tried as much as possible to get outdoors in the summer months, usually going fishing since it not only was an inexpensive sport, but also helped to relieve me of the stress caused by being too busy. La Grande was close to the Wallowa Mountains, where was located some of the best high-lake fishing. I took advantage of the opportunity, hiking up to these hard to get to lakes for a day of fishing for beautiful trout. If the fishing was boring, I would take off exploring, scrambling up steep granite rock formations that overlooked the lakes. I could feel the adrenaline flow as I carefully inched my way up steep, unprotected rock. I loved the feel of the little sharp knobs of the granite under my fingers and palms as I pulled my body over the rocks. Reaching the top, I would just sit and look at the surrounding beauty below me: patches of snow, a green meadow with wild flowers surrounding a lake, and then the pristine water so clear that I could easily see the bottom. It was a wonderful experience and I always dreaded going back to the life in a town. I longed to go out into the mountains more, but unfortunately I was only able to do it a couple of times a year during the few short summer months.

After a little over four years in La Grande, I took a job as an assistant controller with Meier & Frank Co. in Portland, Oregon. While working in Portland, I sat for and passed the national CPA exam and acquired my certification, but I continued to work for the retail company.

I enjoyed working for a large company, wearing a suit and tie, and having a beautiful office with mahogany furniture. The pay was not extraordinary, but at least I was making more than the starvation salary that I had in eastern Oregon. In the same year, 1967, and within a few weeks of passing the CPA exam, we had our second child. This time it was a boy, and we named him Mark.

Living in a large city was exciting, but deep inside I felt a hollowness; something was missing in my life, but I did not know what it was. My job was going well and the company wanted to promote me, but to do so would mean moving back east to a large chain of stores in Ohio, or Pittsburg, Pennsylvania. I could not see moving my young family back east to a manufacturing city, and leaving the beauty of the western states.

One day I received a call from a friend whom I had worked with in the accounting firm in La Grande. He told me that his brother-in-law was acquiring a chain of small to medium size commercial printing companies, and needed a person to fill the position as controller, treasurer and financial officer. The head office was located in Salem, Oregon, just forty-five miles south of Portland. This seemed to be an opportunity to get onto the ground floor of a growing enterprise. They had just acquired their second printing plant and were looking at other expansion. I liked the idea of being involved in a young, progressive organization, and having the opportunity to acquire some ownership as well. I accepted the position, and in September of 1968 moved to Salem.

Salem is a small city, and the location of the state capital. There was nothing strategic about the business being located in Salem, except that it was where the major shareholder acquired the first printing company. We set up a holding corporation to own the acquisitions, and to provide the subsidiary companies management services, as well as to acquire new acquisitions. Initially, there were just three of us in the holding corporation: the President, the head of sales, and myself.

The next five years were fast paced and hectic. We purchased our next twenty- two companies in three years. We grew as fast as we could, but could only grow as fast as our cash flow allowed us since we were a private company and had no outside sources of capital from the sale of stock. Most of my time was spent traveling up and down the west coast, with our most eastern plant located in Salt Lake City, Utah. I was busy setting up accounting controls and training accountants and bookkeepers for each location. I also worked at obtaining bank financing, writing manuals, and providing financial statements for our management team and bankers.

Our President was the majority stockholder, but eight others were allowed to buy minority interests. We developed a five-year business plan, which would enable us to go public, selling stock to outsiders, and providing each of us with a nice retirement.

I enjoyed the work and the responsibility of my position. Even though the travel at first was exciting, I soon became weary of it. Almost every Monday morning, I was at the Portland, Oregon airport catching a flight, and leaving home for a few days. It was usually a trip with more than one stopover. I often woke up in a hotel room wondering where exactly I was. Life seemed to be speeding by, racing to meeting engagements, the airport, then home for a couple of days. It was hard on my family being away so much, so when I was at home I tried to spend most of my time with them. My personal hobbies were almost non-existent, and the only adventures outdoors were family picnics and bicycling around the neighborhood. In 1970, our third child was born. It was a boy and we named him Gregg.

The excitement of business, meeting with bank officers and other professionals in the business world, still left me feeling dissatisfied and empty. Even though I was constantly involved with people, many of them wonderful individuals, there was still a feeling of loneliness. Part of it was that I was not seeing my family enough, but something deeper was bothering me. One's feelings can be very complex; made up of a mixture of many past experiences, beginning when we are small children, all of them funneling into a pool, and creating our individual needs. Some of these needs are certain, and others uncertain, some conscious and others sub-conscious. Quite often we become confused, and even over a lifetime we may never quite figure out what our true needs are. These needs can also change over time, depending on the experiences flowing into the pool. Sometimes we are fortunate, and we zero into exactly what we need in order to satisfy our life at that time. I believed at this time, it was the solitude of nature that I thirsted for. I was in a hectic, social prison, and seemed to have no way to escape.

In 1969 the economy took a sudden and vicious hit. Interest rates went sky high, the stock market dropped, and our country was in a recession. Companies that had grown in giant leaps, without adequate earnings and cash flow were thrown into bankruptcy or near bankruptcy. The availability of borrowed money nearly dried up, mostly available to those businesses that appeared financially secure. Even though we were in the midst of this bad economy, we managed to stay ahead, even acquiring more businesses.

Although our business was built on what we felt was sound management philosophy, we were vulnerable due to the fact that we allowed our subsidiary corporations and their presidents too much autonomy. Because we depended solely on profits for cash flow, leaving us little if any extra capital to back us, it was imperative that we were alerted, and could resolve any cash problems immediately. This meant that we had to have total honesty from all of our management. The reporting controls were installed in each company, but unfortunately we had a couple of dishonest managers whose egos were out of control, and who just plain ignored the reporting requirements and even padded them to hide the problems they had created. The warnings were all there; late and sloppy reporting, excuses and more excuses. Our President was hesitant to move, and by the time we received information from outside third parties as to non-payment of invoices and other debts, we were already in deep financial trouble.

In the summer of 1972, I heard from people around me about how wonderful the mountains near Salem were for hiking and back packing. It sounded fun, and would be a good way to get away from the pressure packed business world for a couple of days. A hike into the Mt. Jefferson Wilderness area sounded especially appealing. I went to the local sporting goods store, purchasing what I thought were the things my wife and I needed for over-night back-packing: tent, sleeping bags, backpacks, stove, pans, etc. Having a few days off in August, my wife and I got a baby sitter for the kids, and headed up to Mt. Jefferson, a six-mile hike into the wilderness, to a location that was supposed to be covered with a meadow and many small lakes, settled below the second highest mountain in Oregon.

The hike in was a wonderful experience, with the fragrance of the alpine forest permeating our senses. I was especially excited at the prospect of seeing for the first time this high mountain settled so far from civilization. The trail was beautiful, but the mountain could not be seen, first, because of a ridge we had to cross over, and then with clouds that had descended down around the mountain before we had a chance to view it.

The low clouds were almost like fog as we hiked down from the surrounding ridge into the area of meadows and lakes. We found a good camp spot at Scout Lake, set up camp, and then prepared our dinner for the evening. As darkness fell, the air became chilly, and soon we were cuddled in our sleeping bags in the small tent. I listened to the sounds outside, so foreign to me: the wind beating on the tent and rustling through the trees, some type of bird sounds, and occasionally the crashing sound of rocks that seemed to be coming from above us.

The next morning I awoke to the sun's rays piercing the flimsy tent. I crawled slowly out of the tent, yawning and stretching my tight muscles. What I saw next just about knocked me over! There, straight in front of me, rising almost four thousand feet higher than our camp was the most gorgeous mountain I had ever seen. It was totally void of clouds, glistening with white glaciers and snow fields, interspersed with giant rock faces, and pinnacles reaching for the sky. My heart nearly stopped! I cannot describe the emotions that quickly ran through me. There was an excitement that I had not experienced for years, and at the same time, a peace and contentment began flowing through me. Could I leave this place, this moment, and never feel it again? Somehow, I had to experience more of it.

Because of the experience in Jeff Park, in the next few weeks I came to a decision that I had to make a change in my life. I felt obligated to the organization and my fellow shareholders to stay until at least adequate financing was arranged. This meant that I would need to be with the company another year or less, depending on how quickly we could obtain loans. Without telling anyone of my decision, I continued to work hard towards the goal of re-financing, spending even more days traveling and meeting with bankers, money brokers, etc. At the same time, I began to discreetly look around for other opportunities.

That Fall I hooked up with a hiking and climbing club from Salem called the Chemeketans. I decided that I would attend their basic climbing course that they offered each spring. That winter I bought the climbing book "A Freedom of the Hills" published by the Seattle Mountaineers and began reading and memorizing parts of it. Also, for a Christmas gift, I received my first set of leather climbing boots.

In late winter, 1972, I rented some crampons and an ice axe, drove to Mt. Hood, and began to explore the upper portions of Mt. Hood, and getting used to my gear. On a nice day in early March, a friend, Bill Marquardt and I decided to see how high we could go alone on Mt. Hood. That day the weather was partially sunny, with clouds blowing by the mountain occasionally obscuring the top. The snow conditions were good, and we worked our way up to Silcox Hut, a small hut located at close to seven thousand feet altitude. We continued upward past the hut, feeling that we could safely turn around anytime and make it back. Soon, we were at 8,300 ft., the top of the Palmer ski lift, which was not running that time of year since it did not open up until spring. One moment the weather would be cloudy, and then clear up. Each time it cleared up, our expectations arose, and we continued on. After a while, I noticed some tracks going up, so we moved over to them. Following them up made the going easier because we could step into the tracks.

We had been watching two climbers ahead of us for quite some time. We seemed to be moving faster, and after a while caught up with them. The two were carrying skis. We chatted, and they told us they were hoping to go to the summit and ski down. At that time and as inexperienced as I was, I thought it to be a little foolish. Neither of them had ever climbed the mountain before, but having more experience than us, we decided to follow them up anyway.

At the 10,400 foot level, there is a narrow steep ridge that runs up a few hundred feet to the large overhanging rocks. This ridge is called the Hog's Back, a place that I was somewhat familiar with, after talking to experienced climbers and reading about the climb. It is the crux section of the standard route on the mountain. It reaches about forty-five degrees in steepness and most of the time has a crevasse running horizontally across it. As we veered around Crater Rock, I got my first view of the Hog's back. I was excited to finally be able to see this obstacle ahead, several hundred feet above us. I could see a few climbers going up the Hog's Back and some of the higher ones were heading towards the small chutes on the side of the large rock face, which led you through the rocks and up the final several hundred feet to the summit. These climbers seemed to be moving very slow. There also came into view some climbers descending at the same time.

After we reached the bottom part of the Hog's Back, we sat down to take a well-earned break. A couple of climbers that had already descended, approached and asked how we were doing. Our two new skier friends mentioned that they were attempting the summit and were hoping to ski down. As the climber turned towards me, I mentioned that I was just up there for the experience of it all, and probably would not be going any further. One of the climbers suggested that we ought to attempt the summit, since the conditions were so good, and the steep section had large steps already kicked. He did not think we needed a rope. We didn't have one anyway.

Bill and I discussed it. He decided that he had gone far enough for this trip, but would wait for me if I wanted to give it a try. I told him that I did. At least try it a short distance up. I proceeded to put on my crampons, the first time ever to wear them. They seemed large and bulky, and I hoped that I would not stab myself with them. Soon, the skier friends got to their feet and began moving up. I threw on my pack and followed. I noticed that the skiers did not have crampons, and I wondered how they would do on the steeper section.

Moving up, we soon came to the crevasse that had a strong looking snow bridge across a two to three foot wide crack. We were soon over that, and heading up the steepening slope. We had large-sized steps kicked by previous climbers to step into, but every few yards one of the skier's feet would slip, and they would nearly fall. Since I was directly below them it filled me with alarm! After happening a few times, one of them turned down toward me and suggested that I go around them, since I was moving faster with crampons on. I was a little concerned about going on my own, as I didn't know how steep it was going to get. I did not want to get into a position where I couldn't handle it. On the other hand, the thought of being below them when someone fell was not very appealing either. I cautiously moved up and around them.

Once I was ahead of them, and with my crampons firmly grasping the snow, I began to feel confident. The adrenaline was really running through my system now, and I began moving at a faster pace even though I was gasping for breath in the thin air. I came to the right side chute and climbed up through it. As soon as I was through, I looked up ahead, and I thought I could see the top of the mountain. It was still a couple of hundred feet higher, but I picked up my pace. I noticed that there weren't other climbers in view. Quite possibly they had all gone down by now. I moved quickly, too quickly, and I had to stop, gasping for air. Then, I was off again, racing to get to the summit. Finally, I could go no further. This was it! The summit! One of the greatest thrills of my life!

I looked around. No one! Just the large, rounded snow covered summit. I moved slowly and carefully towards the edge on the north side and tried to peer over. There was nothing but sky below me.

I remained only a few minutes on the summit, looking over the tremendous beauty and taking pictures. Then, I noticed dark, high clouds beginning to come in towards the mountain. I decided that I had better head down. There was no sign of my companions with the skis. They must have decided not to go to the summit and started their skiing down lower. I carefully ascended, following the tracks that I had come up. Slowly, I went down through the steep chute. I felt something dragging from my left foot, and was horrified to realize that my crampon had come loose and was hanging by the leather strap. I stopped. Thinking over the situation, I decided that it was too steep to try and put it back on. I would just have to go down with one good crampon, dragging the other behind me.

It seemed like it took forever, but finally I was down past the crevasse and onto safer snow. My friend Bill was waiting for me, and as I approached him, he immediately asked if I had made the summit. I answered affirmative, and he was delighted. He would make the climb four months later with me.

I was hooked! I had only set the goal of climbing one major mountain, Mt. Hood, the highest in Oregon. But now all of a sudden, I had goals of climbing as many mountains as possible.

****

I knew that I could never live happily in the busy world that I had for five years. That same year, I became acquainted with the senior partner in a CPA firm located in Monmouth, Oregon. I asked his advice about returning to Pubic Accounting. He told me that I should, and that he would have a job opportunity if and when I decided to leave my present job. The die was cast. I gave notice, and in December, 1973 joined the CPA firm of Fischer and Burton, located in Monmouth, Oregon.

During the next seven years I climbed as often as possible, mostly in the Northwest. I became a climbing leader for a hiking and climbing club, called the Chemeketan's. In 1974, I became a partner in the CPA firm. I also bought a house and six acres in Dallas, Oregon. Life was good, and seemed to move quickly. Then, in 1976 my wife and I obtained a divorce. She moved near Portland, Oregon, taking two of my three children. It was a traumatic time in my life as we had been married fourteen years.

In April, 1976, I met a girl named Jeanne who was working in a bakery near my office. She was also attending college. While chatting with her one day, I found out that she was interested in climbing, and wanted to attend the Chemeketan's annual climbing school. I was in charge of the school that year, and invited her to attend. We were married four months later. I really didn't know her well enough, and

24

after six months of marriage it seemed that I had made a mistake. Our life was full of strife, but we tried to work on the problems, and kept the marriage together. It seemed that the only peaceful times were when we went to the mountains together, away from the pressure, but those times became fewer and fewer.

In 1980, I left the firm (the senior partner had died in 1974) of which I was a partner, and went on my own. Having my own CPA practice was hard and consisted of many hours of work, especially during tax season, but it also afforded me the opportunity to climb when times were slow, or even when a few days were available to escape from the office. Having no children living with me afforded me this extra time. In 1986, a surprise came along. His name was Aaron. Suddenly, with a son in our marriage, life seemed smooth again and full of joy. This happiness would only last a couple of years, and the stress of a bad marriage returned. We turned to counseling, but it didn't help much, except to prolong the inevitable.

Over the years, in addition to my family, work and climbing, I also was involved in charitable work. Among other things, I was able to take two trips to the Mid-East, and one trip to Africa, in order to help the poor and needy. It helped me to be helping others, and seemed to relieve some of the pain of a stressful marriage.

During the ensuing years I continued my climbing. I went on trips to Canada, Mexico and South America to climb, and continued my pursuit of the many peaks in the Northwest, Northern California and Wyoming. Climbing was healing to my spirit, keeping me in close contact with God and nature.

In 1995, the marriage was finished, a real low point in my life. I only made it through this period of time with the grace of God, and the healing effect of his mountains and nature. The divorce was final in March 1998. Some may question whether my many outdoor activities contributed to the two divorces. The answer I believe is no. Both of my failed marriages were with individuals whom both had climbed and loved it. Even though I was gone many times a year, usually for not more than a few days, the remaining time was spent with the family. I tried being close to my wife and kids, and to be a participating parent. Living on six acres of forested land in the country provided the kids many freedoms that other children didn't have. Building tree houses, having ropes to swing across gullies, climbing trees, and raising animals, wasn't the normal life of those living in the cities. The second marriage lasted over twenty years, but probably couldn't have, if it were not for me being able to escape to the mountains to renew my spirit time and time again.

I continue to climb today. It is a basic need of mine. Each summit that I step on, I thank God for the strength, abilities and safety that he gives me. I thank him for the years of experiencing his beautiful and peaceful outdoors. Each of my four children have been able to share with me the summit of more than one major mountain, and I am grateful for that also.

All of us have our **bumps and bruises**. Life is full of them. When as a child, we fall down and no one picks us up, we must pick ourselves up. Each time we pick ourselves up we become stronger and more balanced. Life is also full of peaks and valleys. In order to climb the larger ones, we must first get stronger by climbing the smaller ones. Is the pain and effort worth it? We will not know, until we stand on top of "our summit," and have had the opportunity to experience the fullness of life.

CHAPTER II

MIRACLE ON THE SPUR

I heard what sounded like a rifle shot! I didn't have to guess what it was. My climbing experience had taught me about the dangers involved in doing this kind of sport. Even without looking up, my instincts told me that a large rock had broken away from the ice far above us, and would soon be hurtling down, possibly bringing other rocks, carving away the snow, and creating a snow avalanche.

Avalanches are the most feared of the dangers inherent in mountain climbing. Other dangers can usually be avoided, or protected against, but if an avalanche is coming toward you, you can only pray that it will miss you. You cannot move fast enough to get out of harm's way on a slope as steep as the one we were on. I wasn't so fearful of being covered over by snow and debris, but rather being swept off the nearly sixty degree slope to the glacier two thousand feet below us.

I quickly looked up, and true enough the large boulders and rocks were rolling down the side of the mountain towards us, some hurtling like a gymnast in an Olympic competition, slicing the snow each time they connected. It would be just a matter of seconds, and the rocks would be upon us. We were right in the same area where almost all avalanches set their course on this route. I had no time to think about dying, only time to put my body as close to the steep slope as possible and wait to get hit.

How did two mountaineers with many years of training get themselves into a position like this? We knew that this route was considered a "killer" having claimed many lives over the years. Many of the deaths had been caused by carelessness, some by plain inexperience, and yet some were by just plain bad luck. I remember most of them, having read about them in newspaper accounts, or talking to people that were involved in the rescue operations to retrieve their bodies. Because of the reputation of this route, Bob and I had planned on making this as safe a climb as possible. We were well experienced, and thought we had a logical strategy for doing the climb. But nonetheless, here we were, hopelessly waiting for what fate had in store for us.

To understand how we got ourselves into this situation, we need to go back a few days to the beginning of the story.

****

"Hey Robert, looks like the weather is finally beginning to break. Supposed to clear up and be nice on Monday."

From the other end of the phone I heard, "Is that right? When do you want to go for it?"

"The weather's to be iffy on Sunday, then the storm is moving through and projected to be beautiful on Monday. Of course, you know how you can trust the weatherman in this State!"

"That's for sure!" Both Bob and I knew how inaccurate weather predictions were, especially on mountains located in the Northwest, near the coast.

"I'm a little concerned about the fresh snow the last couple of weeks, but hopefully it has consolidated enough to be safe. The freezing level is supposed to remain fairly low, so that will help!"

"Sounds good to me! Let's go for it!" Bob sounded motivated, but not overly excited, but that was my "laid back" friend. After over twenty years of climbing, it would take more than just another climb up Oregon's tallest mountain to get any excitement out of him.

"How about driving up to Hood on Sunday, and then hike up to base camp on Cooper Spur ridge in the afternoon? We'll go for the summit on Monday."

"Good idea! We'll also miss a crowded summit since it will be Monday."

I agreed, hoping that we would enjoy the summit entirely by ourselves. Perhaps it was selfish on my part, but I relished the thought of a *true wilderness experience* without a crowd. Maybe I was being a little optimistic since Mt. Hood is the second most climbed mountain in the world, ranking only behind Mt. Fuji in Japan. But then again, this was not the standard route up the mountain.

Mt. Hood is a serene, and most of the year, ice and snow covered peak, rising majestically 11,239 feet above sea level. It looks down like a sentinel from the port city of Portland, Oregon, less than sixty miles away. From a distance, the mountain looks to be a very formidable object to climb because of its many glaciers, and the startling steepness. The pioneers who first passed this way in their wagon trains thought that the white towering giant would never be climbed. Because of its location with easy accessibility, it is a favorite among mountaineers, "peak baggers," and even beginning climbers. From Portland, one can drive up to Timberline Lodge, located on the south side of the mountain, in just a few hours. The lodge is located at approximately 6,000 feet, where most parties don their climbing gear, and then head up to climb a number of available routes. The most popular of these routes is the south side route, which takes you directly through the broken crater and then to the summit.

Bob and I had chosen another, less climbed ridge on the north eastern side of the mountain, named "Cooper Spur." Even though this route was frequently climbed, it had the reputation of being a "killer," because of the many deaths occurring on it over the years. Even during my years of climbing, I could remember at least a dozen people dying on it. It seemed to claim lives almost yearly, with the greatest tragedy coming in 1981 when two rope teams, while descending Cooper Spur, slipped on the soft ice just below the summit, sending them sliding, and then hurtling over three thousand feet to the Elliot Glacier below. Of the seven climbers, two miraculously lived, but five died, sending a chill through the climbing world. Today, on the ridge at approximately 9,000 feet, there is a memorial to this tragic event. A bronze plaque listing the five climbers that died is attached to what is called "Tie-In Rock." This is a large rock, located at the point on the ridge where climbing parties fasten their climbing harnesses to the climbing rope, before heading up the steep obstacle ahead. The memorial is a vivid reminder of what can be in store above.

Not only is the next 2,000 feet steep and exposed, with one section reaching sixty degrees in steepness, it's also prone to avalanche and rock fall. Early in the morning, as the warming sun touches the eastern slopes of snow and ice, the softening can bring down the unconsolidated snow. Higher up, the melting ice loosens rotten rock, sometimes sending it hurtling and crashing down the exposed routes. Even under the most ideal conditions, climbers are prone to be peppered by small rock fall. This rock, falling at remarkable speeds from near the summit is often triggered only by gusting winds.

In my opinion, the most dangerous part of the climb occurs on the descent from the summit. Not only is the upper portion steep and terribly exposed, but once the sun touches it, the ice softens, and descending can be compared to coming down on soft "butter." The placing of some type of protection such as ice screws becomes meaningless. If slipping or falling, the only chance for survival is by instantly going into "self-arrest," driving the ice axe into the ice, while kicking in the toes of the boots. Even then, if the snow is too soft, this act is hopeless. It is usually under these conditions that descending climbers have paid the "ultimate price."

I had made up my mind, that because of the problems of descending, the only way I wanted to climb this route was by carrying all the gear to the summit, and then descending a safer route. Two years prior, I had led this climb and that's exactly what we did. We left some transportation at Timberline Lodge on the south side, and then car-pooled over to the trailhead on the east side of the mountain. Except for the inconvenience of using extra vehicles, climbing the steep route with a heavy pack, then lugging it the three and a quarter miles from the summit to the lodge, it enabled us to have a safe descent. In my mind, safety and peace of mind more than offset the very physical aspect of doing it this way. Besides, I considered it great conditioning for the larger mountains.

On Sunday morning we drove to Timberline Lodge, left one vehicle there, then had my family drive Bob and I to the trailhead on the east side at Tilly Jane Park. Tilly Jane Campground is located on the east side of the mountain, in thick trees, and where we will begin hiking up the flanks of the mountain that will connect us with the spur. It is located just a few hundred feet lower than the tree line. Normally in the summer months it is packed with campers, hikers, and climbers, but since the weather had been poor up until now, it was deserted. Most of the snow had melted away by this time, but it was too early for the wild flowers and forest foliage to be in bloom. It was a cold and damp place, showing the effects of a long and cold winter.

Upon reaching the park, I immediately opened the trunk and we began sorting out the packs and climbing gear. Even though the weather was cloudy, with only the lower slopes of the mountain visible, we were in great spirits. We talked and joked as we went through the frequent ritual of adding weight to our packs. Just the smell of the trees and inhaling the fresh mountain air was enough to exhilarate our moods. Suddenly, it dawned on me that something important was missing among our gear. The rope! We had forgotten to bring the rope!

I embarrassingly said, "Bob, guess what?" He looked up at me curiously. I continued, "We forgot the rope!" I used the term "we," hoping to share the blame with my climbing partner.

"The Hell we did, Bob grumbled!" After a few seconds of silence, he added, "What do we do now?"

I knew Bob wasn't angry. He wasn't likely to get upset over such a thing. We had both done similar things in the past. A few years prior we had forgotten the climbing rope after driving for a day and a half to the North Cascades to climb Forbidden Peak. Fortunately, we were able to buy one from the Rangers at the U.S. Ranger Station nearby, otherwise it would have been a long, depressing drive home. Still, it would be sad to drive home after this effort. Worse of all, we wouldn't be able to climb.

"I sure in the heck don't want to go home", I said, with a tone showing disgust at myself for such a stupid oversight.

I could feel my face flushing from the embarrassment. How did I forget the rope? Did I not use my checklist? I always tried to run through my home made check sheet, ticking off the important items as I got my gear together. In addition to the ice axe and crampons, the rope is the most important devise used by the climber. Climbing without a rope on most climbs is like a scuba diver diving without his buddy and an auxiliary air supply. It's also like a parachutist not having a safety chute. I thought "parachutist." Parachute cord! That's it! Why not use parachute cord?

"Bob, I've got an idea! We can use parachute cord for our rope." Reaching into the side pocket of my pack I pulled out a small bundle of red cord. "I try to always carry extra cord just in case of emergency. This should work, if we have enough."

"But that won't be enough to make a rope", replied Bob.

"We can use the guy lines from the tent also. This stuff has about 1,000 lbs. tensile strength, and by doubling it, or even tripling it, it should be strong enough to hold a fall."

"You're pretty sure of that?" Bob did not sound too convinced.

I continued, "Any fall would be more than likely a slip, which wouldn't require great strength in a rope." Of course I wasn't thinking about a fall into a crevasse, but we should only have one crevasse on the descent to worry about, and normally it did not present a problem. "What do you think?'

"Oh well, why not? We aren't going to fall anyway," he answered in a more positive tone.

My wife and son had been taking in this whole scenario with mild amusement, believing that we would eventually decide to head home. Instead, we began slipping on our packs.

Bob asked, "What about the helmets?"

I thought for a few seconds about it, remembering how much I loathed wearing a helmet. I had begun my climbing in the days that climbing helmets were only occasionally worn. You'd never see the skilled "Yosemite" big wall climbers wearing them. Helmets were less than comfortable, and even though they had vent holes, you never really could feel the air rushing through your hair. "You know, since we brought the darn things all the way up here, let's go ahead and put them on our packs." Little did I know at the time how much that decision would affect the outcome of the climb.

We said good-bye to my family, and then headed out with our heavy loads.

****

We walked through the Tilly Jane campground, winding our way up through the trees and heading for the tree line. I was anxious to get through the dark trees and into the open area. Looking ahead, excitement began to flow through my body as I tried to make out some features of the mountain.

As I left the trees, and started up a rock and grass gully, I could see the ridge still several hundred feet above me. I headed for an area that had less scree on it so I would have better footing approaching the ridge. I could see that the mountain was still obscured by clouds. I was looking forward to getting on the ridge where I would have a better view of the glacier lying on the other side. The temperature was cool, being perfect for the upcoming physical exertion. Even though the pack was heavy, it felt good on my back. It was

34

like an old friend to me. There is something special in knowing that your life sustaining possessions are on your back with you. Without the various items of clothing, food and equipment, your stay in the mountains would be for a very short period of time. In many situations, your survival utterly depends on some or all of these items. The pack gave me a feeling of security, knowing that regardless of the conditions encountered on a mountain, your survival was almost assured.

With the feeling of excitement running through me, I unknowingly had taken off at a very quick pace, and could now feel my lungs beginning to burn, and the legs to weaken.

I needed to slow down, and get into a comfortable rhythm. All experienced climbers and hikers are familiar with setting a rhythm, insuring that exhaustion doesn't set in later at the higher altitudes where the air is much thinner. I stopped and quickly glanced back to see how far Bob was behind me. I was beginning to leave him behind. I missed his joking and funny comments, and even cursing sometimes depending on his mood.

I had climbed with Bob for over eighteen years. Of the many climbers that I had climbed with, Bob was my favorite. He was a tall, lanky guy, and a few years older than me. He was well liked and got along with almost everyone, with his laid-back and humorous personality. We hit it off as friends the first time we met. He was an assistant leader on one of my first year climbs that I signed up for with a climbing club. Even though the climb was a little scary for a novice like me, he made me feel comfortable with his easygoing assurance. I am a more serious type individual, but he is a person that can keep me in stitches during most of a trip. Even though he usually took things in stride, rarely seeming to get rattled, if he did become annoyed over something, he could curse a "blue streak." Once in a while, these annoyances could be something very little, such as dropping a fork between some rocks that he was sitting on while eating. A torrent of foul words could fill the air. Even during these moments, he would still make you laugh.

We also had many things in common to "BS" about, during our many hours on a mountain. He loved sports and military history, two subjects that I loved also. We could spend our time playing our version of "sports trivia," with questions like "Who were the players making up the "Steel Curtain" on the famous Pittsburgh Steeler's football team of the eighties?" Bob had a tremendous memory for all sports that far exceeded mine, but I was still capable of stimulating his memory with good questions. He was such a sports fan that he usually carried a tiny transistor radio and would listen to any game whether it was high school, college, pro or even little league, usually in the comfort of his sleeping bag. Soon he would be snoring. Later I could wake him, and he would still tell me the score, then fall back to sleep. Once on a climbing trip to Mexico he listened to a local soccer game. Whether or not he knew what was going on, I'll never know.

Bob and I shared other things as well, such as family, our spiritual beliefs, and plans for the future, but usually we just kept things simple between us, enjoying the beauty and freedom of the outdoors together. Like so many climbers, special moments of the time can be shared by just remaining silent and enjoying the environment around you.

The weather continued cool and cloudy, and in less than an hour I had gained the ridge. Still, only the lower portion of the mountain could be seen. I was at a point where I could now look down the other side of the ridge to the broken up glacier below me, with the many crevasse's now exposed, and peppered with rock fall that had come down from high above. As I gazed at the glacier, the larger rocks looked like people actually on the glacier, and if you stared at the rocks long enough, it seemed as if they were moving, and sometimes peering into the deep frozen crevices below. I knew these were not people, for I had seen these mirage type scenes before on other climbs, especially late in the evening and after exhaustion had set in. I recall a time on Mt. Rainier when my friends and I actually argued about what these people were doing on the glacier far below us after staring at them for minutes, only to find out the next day that it was only rocks that we had seen.

I stopped, adjusted the pack on my shoulders, all the while hoping to see through the clouds and the steep upper portion of our climb. I was now approximately at the eight thousand foot level on the ridge, and I could see ahead to where the ridge turned directly into the mountain. Looking further along the ridge, I could make out a large rock sitting directly in the middle of the ridge, at a spot where the ridge seemed to level off for a short distance. I guessed that this was the place where we would place our tent and spend the night. From where I was standing, I estimated I had around eight hundred feet elevation gain remaining to that spot, and should be there in thirty minutes. Again, I felt the excitement of being on the mountain. I took a few sips of water from my water bottle, and then after a few deep breaths of the cool, moist air, began heading up again.

A slight but cold breeze began blowing in my face as I moved up the rock ridge. It felt good, and I was hoping that it would stay cool, keeping the snow firm and limiting any rock fall on tomorrows steep climbing. At the present there wasn't any sound of rock fall, which was a normal thing to occur during late afternoons and evenings. The only sound that I could hear was the crunch of the rocks under my feet as I took each step. I was thinking that if only the clouds would clear before darkness set in so that we could get a good view of our route, and enjoy the final moments of the day at our camp high on Cooper Spur.

It was around 6:00 p.m. as I approached the large rock and our potential bivouac site. As I walked into the camp area, I noticed that the snow had partially melted away, leaving a bare spot large enough to place our tent near the rock. I quickly took off my pack, carefully placing it to the side so I could start clearing the rocks away from the area that our tent and sleeping bags would be. As I cleared the rocks, I alternated looking up ahead to see if the clouds on the upper slopes were clearing, then back down the ridge from where I had just come from to see if Bob was in sight yet.

It took only a few minutes to clear the rocks. As I was unpacking my portion of the tent, I glanced again down the ridge, and just coming into view was the top of Bob's head and then his entire body as he turned the corner on the ridge. I pulled out the stove and prepared it to light so we would save time in preparing our meal.

A short while later Bob came slowly into camp and proceeded to drop his pack. "Well, *sheee iiite!*" A favorite expression of his. Then, plopping down on the edge of the snow, "This is quite the spot! I believe the dictionary calls this an *aerie*, or some darn thing like that. Pretty damn impressive I would say!"

"Yep. Not as spiffy as the Hilton, but a lot more beautiful," I replied.

Bob, after glancing around in all directions, "Man! This sucker drops off on both sides!"

He wasn't kidding. Next to us, the north side of the ridge dropped sharply over a thousand feet down to the Elliot Glacier. On the other side, there was a steep snowfield angling down an equal distance. Our tent spot was situated on the ridge just between these two drop-offs, with around twelve to fifteen feet to operate. This was plenty of room for two *old goats.*

"Yeah Bob! I hope that neither of us walk in our sleep tonight."

"That's for damn sure!"

We quickly set up the tent, anchoring the guy-lines sufficiently with some larger rocks. After throwing our pads and sleeping bags inside, we went about the business of preparing our food.

"What's on the menu tonight, Bob?"

"Good old Chili Mac," came his reply. He added, "The gourmet's delight." Then after a little more thought, "I'm not sure that it is a good idea since I had lasagna last night."

"Gourmet's delight is right! With that combination, I'll probably need to call you the *galloping gourmet.*" After chuckling, I continued, "I guess I'm just having plain old beef stew." I added, "I did bring a surprise for our after dinner dessert."

"The heck you did? What'd you bring?"

"You remember that stuff that Brownlee literally ate all the way up McKinley? Without waiting for an answer I continued, "Its freeze dried *amaretto cheese cake*. I ordered it through the catalog."

"Hell of a deal!" responded Bob with new enthusiasm. Bob was always available to try new food items. He was a big man, with an even bigger appetite.

Watching Bob prepare dinner was a delight in itself. Constantly talking to himself, as if going through some kind of ritual, it was as if this exercise actually improved the quality of the food. He sustained the same exuberance when eating it also, with the expression looking like each bite to be a treasure to his palate. Freeze dried food was good, but never that good.

As we were eating, the clouds began to lift, slowly revealing the steep portion of the ridge ahead of us.

Excitedly, "Hey Bob, look at that! There's our route for tomorrow." After a pause, "It really doesn't look too bad."

"Looks steep enough," Bob replies in a hesitant tone. Then he asks, "Do we head straight up?"

"Yeah, the route is pretty straight forward. About midway up the first steep area, just above the avalanche debris, we veer to the right towards those exposed rocks. That's the steepest part of the climb, probably reaching around sixty degrees. After that, there is less steepness, but with much more exposure on the other side."

A couple of hundred yards up past "Tie-In Rock" we could see the remains of a small avalanche. We would have to thread our way through the ice chunks, rocks and piled up snow. There was probably a large accumulation of snow during the last couple of weeks, and it concerned me that it had avalanched under such cold conditions, and it lay directly in our path. But, if it remained as cold as it was, and with an early start, we should be up past the more exposed area before the sun's rays begun touching it. The key was a very early start in the morning to avoid the sun.

The mountain continued to clear, and after dinner the upper portion of the mountain was completely clear. Only the valley below us still had clouds, but even these could be seen moving east, like an immense river with waves. The setting sun, shining at an angle, was giving the clouds multiple colors of yellow and orange.

Pulling out his camera Bob began taking pictures. He commented on the scenery below, "This is what makes climbing really worthwhile."

I agreed, and thought about how fortunate we were to view a scene of beauty such as this. Only mountaineers get to spend adequate time absorbing such beauty and tranquility, truly a gift from God. We must have spent a half hour or more looking at the scenery below, chatting about past climbs, and climbs to come. Off to the north, you could see the Cascade giants protruding out of the clouds: Adams, St. Helens and Mt. Rainier. In two weeks, both Bob and I were leading climbs up Mt. Rainier, each by a different route, hoping to meet on the summit. Bob would be leading the Emmons Glacier route, and I the Kautz route. We hadn't even finished this climb and here we were thinking about the next one already.

The mountain hid the sun from us, and as it settled in the west, a stiff cold breeze came up. We hurried to finish putting things away for the night, and then crawled into the tent and our warm sleeping bags. In only moments, my body was warmed by the cozy sleeping bag. As I lay, listening to the rustle of the wind against the tent, I thought about how fortunate I was to have this hobby. I was truly a blessed person, having climbed for so many years. During this time there had been no major accidents to either my climbing partners or me. Sure, there had been some close calls, and I had been trapped in storms a couple of times, but these things can be expected if you climb often enough. No one can truly predict the weather, or the conditions on a mountain. Using your wisdom and common sense helps, but mountains and conditions change daily, even hourly, which is a major part of the challenge in climbing.

I have what I consider a wonderful security, even far more than my skills and knowledge in climbing. I trust in God, and believe that prayer is my greatest security. God had brought me through desperate situations in the past, not only in climbing, but also in other areas of my life. I feel that the help that I received was truly God's miracles. Some may believe these happenings to be the result of "luck or fate," but I believe in "Divine Intervention." Many others besides myself have survived near tragic experiences, and a great number attribute their survival to help from a "Higher Power." I also believe in that, and believe this "Higher Power" to be the Lord, and only the Lord. On each climb, before I doze off at night, I ask the Lord for special protection and the wisdom to do what is right, not only for me, but for my climbing partners, and believing that he has heard me, will answer my prayers. I know that his answers may not always be exactly the way I want things, but will work out according to his divine will. This evening was no different. I prayed, and then went into a deep, peaceful sleep.

As I awoke, I was startled by the fact that it was already light out, and the temperature unusually warm for being that high on a mountain. I quickly realized that we had over slept. Looking at my watch, I was chagrined to see it was six a.m. rather than the four a.m. that I had planned on in order to break camp and start up the mountain before the warm sun touched the steep slopes above. More alarming, was that apparently the weatherman was wrong again, and the freezing level was much higher than the forecasted eight thousand feet.

"Bob, rise and shine! We've over slept!"

Bob, alerted by the anxiousness in my voice quickly glanced at his watch. "Holy Cow! It's past six already!"

Quickly putting on the outer clothes over my long johns I exclaimed, "We need to get going up this ridge as fast as possible after getting a little food in us. I'm afraid the sun will be touching the mountain soon." The only reason that the sun was not touching it at this time was because of a few clouds in the east blocking it.

"It shouldn't take long to break camp since we are practically already packed," Bob suggested.

"Yes, but we still need to get the guy lines off the tent in order to put together our climbing rope. Bob, why don't you heat some water quickly for oatmeal, tea or whatever, and I'll work on the rope."

I quickly finished putting on my boots, then a jacket and cap and crawled out of the tent. The weather was beautiful! The sun was just beginning to hit our little bivouac site. I looked up at the steep climb ahead and quickly tried to calculate where we would be in approximately two hours. Probably a little lower than the steepest portion, near the crux of the climb. We should be past that section by now. I was angry with myself for over sleeping, as the warm conditions concerned me. It was time to hurry!

We quickly ate, and while having some hot tea began putting the gear into our packs. With the tent cord, and the additional parachute cord that I had available for emergencies, I was able to put together a rope made up of three strands approximately thirty-five feet in length.

"Well Bob, I'm sure glad Hank Keeton told me the story of how during an emergency situation he had been forced to rappel down a rock face using just a single strand of parachute cord, otherwise, I would have never thought of it."

"By the way, that was the *late* Hank Keeton," Bob replied sarcastically. He added, "I'm sure this would really impress our students in the climbing school on safe climbing."

I chuckled and replied, "But Bob, it is called innovation."

It was around eight a.m. as we put on our crampons, then clipped into the very funny looking red rope, and started up the slope. Within ten minutes we had reached "Tie-In Rock." We paused for a moment and read the memorial plaque with the names of the five climbers who had fallen to their deaths nearly ten years earlier. I tried to block out the image of such a disaster, but I could feel my heart beat faster and the adrenalin begin to flow.

After "Tie-In Rock" the steepness increased, and my breathing came with more effort as I adjusted to the thinner air and the strain of the heavy pack on my body. The first half hour always seems the toughest part of climbing, especially early in the morning. After sleeping on hard ground all night, the body is stiff, with the blood not yet fully circulated to the legs and lower body. The lungs seem tight, fighting to inhale the air sufficiently into the lower part of the lungs. Soon though, I had found the rhythm, and my body began to move like it should; a finely tuned up engine.

We worked our way through the avalanche debris quickly and were soon back on solid footing, although the top of the ice seemed to be getting soft. A few yards further, we stopped for a moment, looking down at our bivouac site, and appreciating what a beautiful spot it was.

Looking down at Bob, "We seem to be moving at a good pace, considering the heavy packs that we are lugging. Man, I'll really feel good though when we get past that next section ahead, with the way this snow is softening."

Bob didn't answer, but I could see him nod in agreement as he tried taking in a few extra gulps of air before continuing up.

The slope was now reaching nearly fifty degrees in steepness, and I began kicking in deeper steps, making it easier for Bob, by giving him good footing. My crampons were getting through the soft snow into the ice, providing me good footing, and as my ice axe bit into the ice firmly above me, I felt secure climbing under these conditions. We were to the left and a few yards below the steepest section of the climb. I had been angling to the left, zigzagging as it is called, and about to begin angling to the right, which would bring me to the sixty-degree section. This next steep section is perhaps fifty to a hundred feet long, and once past it the ridge lessens in steepness. I looked forward to the easier and safer upper slopes.

****

Now, here we were, in harm's way, with boulders, rocks and snow racing down upon us. I yelled at Bob, "Avalanche!" I was grasped by fear, as I knew we had no place to go! It was too steep, and there was no time to move. With my ice axe clawing the slope with my left hand, I quickly placed my helmet against the ice, and raised my right hand above me to ward off the falling rocks. I could feel the cold ice on the side of my face as I clung to the slope, hoping to get close enough that the rocks would bounce over me, missing my body. My greatest concern was getting knocked off my stance, falling and taking Bob with me a couple of thousand feet to the Elliot Glacier below. Small rocks began peppering my body. I waited! A larger one hit my right hand, which I had placed above me, tearing flesh off my knuckle. Then it all stopped! I pulled my head back from the slope and looked down to my right to see if Bob was okay. He looked all right and seemed to be prepared, braced the best he could be for a fall. I quickly glanced at my hand and saw that the knuckle was torn and bleeding. No big deal! I could survive that.

I was just beginning to recover my breath when Bob yelled, "Gary, a *big one is coming right at you!*" My heart leapt into my throat! I had never heard Bob with panic in his voice before, and I knew that it must be serious. Without looking up, I again clung to the slope, bracing for what was heading directly for me. Was my time up?

It's amazing the thoughts that go quickly through your mind in a matter of mille-seconds. I certainly didn't want my life to end now. There were so many things that I still wanted to do in life. Life was exciting for me, and I wanted to experience much more of that excitement, yet, I now had no control over my life. At this moment and place, my life was in God's hands completely, and I knew that the outcome would be totally according to his will.

It was sudden, and felt as if a sledgehammer had hit my helmet! I saw stars as a result of the blow, and since I was facing downward, I glimpsed the rock as it flew over my body. It was large, perhaps three feet long, six to eight inches thick, and colored rusty brown. It was unimaginable that I was hit with that size of a rock! My ears were ringing, and I was afraid to move because I didn't yet know the extent of the damage to my head. I continued clinging to the slope.

The next thing I heard was, "Gary! Are you okay?"

I slowly answered, "I believe so Bob. My ears are still ringing though."

Bob was below and to my right, just barely thirty feet away, and yet he seemed untouched by the rock fall. "Take it easy, and don't try to move too soon," he instructed.

He was right. I had heard stories of injured climbers on steep slopes standing up too soon, only to fall again, this time to their death.

"I believe that I'm okay now. I'll try standing up straight," I added, knowing that he would brace himself in case I collapsed.

I slowly pushed myself away from the slope. Just then, another sound above us, a slight roar, and we both looked up in time to see the snow part of the avalanche descending on us. It was not a large avalanche, but had enough snow and speed to knock both of us off our feet. Without even speaking we quickly raised our parachute cord rope between us, extending our arms as high as possible. The two foot deep cascade of snow roared between us, clear of our rope, and just inches from our feet. Our quick reaction had saved our lives, keeping us from being swept off the mountain.

At this point, my heart was really pounding. We just stood for a few seconds astounded at what had just occurred. At the same time we followed with our eyes the fast moving avalanche of snow and debris crashing further and further below us until it disappeared out of sight. We both knew then, how close we had come to death.

"*Whoa!*" I yelled out. Then swallowing hard, I said to Bob, "I'm okay, just a headache. I continued, "I think we should head up this thing quickly."

Bob replied, "Maybe we should head down. Another one could break loose."

I really didn't want to head down, especially with the possibility of rocks coming down the back of us. I felt that if we could just make it another hundred feet, we would be out of the line of fire, and I told Bob so. More than that, a calming peace was beginning to settle inside me. It was a feeling hard to describe, and one that I had experienced only a few times in my life. I felt an assurance that no harm would come to us. I was determined not to surrender to *fear*. I quickly made up my mind! We were heading up!

"Bob, we don't have far to go, and we'll be out of the line of fire, maybe another hundred feet. Let's move up as fast as we can!"

"All right, if you think so," he replied as if hesitant. Possibly he felt that my mind wasn't functioning properly due to the blow on the head that I had taken, but as I headed up, he followed behind me anyway.

I now felt total confidence that we had nothing to fear. There was joy in my heart knowing that a miracle had just occurred. Sure, one could say that the helmet had taken the force of the glancing blow and saved my life, but the rock could have easily torn my head off. What about the snow roaring between us that could have easily swept us down the mountain? This wasn't just *luck* or *fate*. No! I believed that it was the answer to prayer for our safety, and I thanked the Lord for sparing our lives.

It's amazing the energy that adrenaline gives you when pumping through your system. Even though we were on the steepest portion of the climb and carrying packs over fifty pounds, my body felt like it was barely exerting itself. We were soon past the crux of the climb, and then climbing on the portion of the ridge that lessened in steepness and gave us a direct line to the summit. The rest of the way would be much easier climbing, and it looked to be free of any rock hazard.

As we ascended the last several hundred feet up Cooper Spur, I kept thinking about how great it was to be alive. It was a perfectly clear day, and although a little warm now, there was just enough of a breeze to keep it from being unbearable. It was good to be *breathing pure air.* Even though the slope had lessened to forty-five degrees, I made sure that each step I took was well planted, and that my ice axe was firmly in place before going to my next step. We were now in the area where soft slick snow had caused most of the fatal accidents in the past. No sense being foolish now. Even though I trusted in Bob's abilities, I was still going to make good tracks for Bob to step into.

Upon reaching the cornice, which is the overhanging ice that ran along the final summit ridge, I proceeded to a section that had the least overhang. Sometimes, cornices (the overhanging side of a ridge) can be so large that they are impossible to climb through. Using my ice axe, I reached up and worked at cutting away a section of the cornice large enough to allow my body to squeeze through. I was slammed with cold snow as a large section of the cornice fell on me. I climbed up into the cut-away section, then reached up and jammed the pick of my ice axe into the snow above, pulling my way up out of the notch to the top. Upon gaining the top, I drove the ice axe into the snow as far as I could, then using my boot to brace it, slid the rope around the ice axe, and began belaying Bob up to me. A few minutes later Bob was squeezing up through the cut out section of the cornice. As he grunted his way up through it, I extended my hand to him, welcoming him to the summit ridge.

"We did it partner! Welcome to the summit."

"We sure as hell did!" replied Bob, followed by a *Wahoooo*!

We stood there for a moment, catching our breath and staring down at the route we had just come up. An amazing site!

"I don't know why we do such crazy things, but I guess someone's got to do it," Bob exclaimed.

I laughed at what Bob said. I had heard this same comment many many times before, and would probably hear it again and again.

As we casually headed up the last hundred feet to the true summit, it suddenly dawned on me that we were the only ones up here. This was truly remarkable, since there is usually dozens of climbers scattered around the summit. Finally, we were on the summit. We stopped, shook hands, then dropped our packs, and began taking in the surrounding beauty. It was a perfectly clear day, and you could see all the peaks of the Cascade Range, both north and south of us.

We soon had our water and food out. With all of the excitement happening below, we had not bothered to drink or eat for several hours. I didn't realize how thirsty and hungry I was until I started refreshing myself. We nibbled on gorp, cheese and crackers, candy bars, and anything else we could find in our packs. After thirty or forty minutes of lying around eating and resting our bodies, we decided it was time to head down. We struggled to our feet, and again lifted the heavy packs onto our shoulders.

****

I was now aware of how heavy my pack was, and how my body was rebelling to be carrying it again as I headed down the soft snow from the summit. It would take from two to three hours to descend the three miles to Timberline Lodge where our vehicle was parked. We were descending the "standard" route, which is the easiest route on the mountain. Except for going down a forty to forty-five degree ramp called the "Hogs Back," followed by the bergschrund, or main crevasse, that usually ran across the lower part of the ramp, it was a pretty straight-forward and safe descent route. We still had to be careful though since experienced climbers know that most accidents occur on the descent. These accidents usually occur due to exhaustion, but can also be due to *throwing caution to the wind*. I had been guilty a few times in the past of not being cautious, but fortunately the results were just a scare; a "wake up call," and I was determined not to be suckered into it again.

Down through the "Pearly Gates" we went, a small chute located on the side of a large over-hanging rock, which now was covered with ice. Next was the steep ramp, or "Hogs Back," and we slowly made our way cautiously down it. The "Hog's Back" is fairly wide at the top, but drops off five to six hundred feet down its steep sides. As you descend, it narrows until you have only a couple of feet of leeway on each side of you. Taking a fall here can be quite dangerous. Not only can you slide and tumble a long distance, but there's also the chance of falling into the crevasse.

The snow was building up under my crampons now, and I had to take time to stop and knock it loose with my ice axe to prevent slipping. The snow was very soft, and every few steps my foot would break out of the step, nearly causing me to fall. I kept my body low and close to the snow placing my ice axe below me so that if I slipped, I could immediately go into self-arrest. Since we had not climbed up this route, I wasn't quite sure where the *shrund* or crevasse was located, nor the condition would it be in. Sometimes, it presented a mere step-over, but other times it can be a major obstacle, forcing climbers to traverse far to the right or left on steep terrain until you find a place to go around it. Other times, an adequate snow bridge is available to walk over, with the chasm or hole directly beneath you.

As I looked down below me, I could now see that the crevasse was wide open, and extended quite a distance to both the right and the left of the ramp. Was there a snow bridge available? I was hoping so, because the traverse above the crevasse looked to be dangerous, especially on soft snow, and at this point I could not see where the crevasse ended.

Reaching the crevasse, I peered into the blue, icy depths below, and guessed it was at least fifty feet deep. I glanced back and forth looking for a traverse, and saw that the crevasse reached nearly vertical rock formations on both ends. Not a good situation!

I yelled back at Bob, "Do you see any place to cross this thing?"

"Looks like there might be a snow bridge way to the right. Do you see it?"

I glanced in the direction that he indicated, and could make out what looked like a very thin snow bridge. As I was looking at it, I noticed a climber approaching the crevasse from below, heading towards the bridge. Possibly he was following the route up and over the crevasse. I decided to check it out closer, so I headed down and then traversed across to the snow bridge. I was hoping that it would look safer once I got closer. I was very concerned about the soft snow, and the possibility of the snow bridge collapsing if I tried to cross over, especially with the heavy pack that I was carrying. As I came close to the snow bridge, I realized that it looked to be in worse condition than I had expected. Again, looking both directions, I felt that probably the only option was to try it.

The climber on the other side was now just standing there watching me as I inched closer. He took out his camera, possibly hoping to get a dramatic picture if I fell through, which was a little unnerving to me. As I stood next to the thin bridge, I recalled the events of the day. We had survived a rock and snow avalanche, hadn't we? Again, the assurance that I had felt after the avalanche began to flow into me. I made up my mind, I was going to cross!

"Bob, put me on a boot-axe belay! I'm going for it!" The belay, in soft snow conditions is questionable to say the least. It was a difficult maneuver, and to be effective it required firm snow conditions. We didn't have these conditions, but at least it gave me a little psychological support, feeling that possibly Bob could hold me if I broke through the bridge.

Bob soon responded, "Belay on! Go for it, and good luck!"

I gingerly took my first step. It held but the bridge was fragile! It was eerie looking, and I could see small openings in it. I hoped that it was still frozen solid underneath the soft top layer, due to the previous days of cold weather. I took the next step, ever so easy! Another step! Then another! I took each step very carefully as if I was walking on broken glass. Soon, I had crossed the ten to twelve foot gap, and now was standing on firm snow. I breathed a sigh of relief! Now to get Bob across! I moved away from the crevasse a few yards, and then set up my own boot-axe belay.

"Okay Robert! Your turn! Tread softly my friend!"

"Thanks a lot!" came the somewhat sarcastic reply from Bob. Bob moved forward, and soon his six foot five inch body, and heavy pack were across.

"It's a piece of cake the rest of the way," I happily commented.

All the while, the lone climber had been watching these events. I asked him, "Are you planning on going to the summit? If so, I would be extra careful crossing that snow bridge."

He responded, "No thanks! It's too scary for me. I think I'll just stop here for a while and take in the sights. By the way, which route did you guys climb?"

I explained that we had climbed up the "Cooper Spur" route on the east side of the mountain. When he asked how that had gone, I briefly explained to him about the avalanche.

He responded, "Doesn't sound like something that I would have wanted to do. Matter of fact, it sounds pretty darn dangerous!"

We stood and chatted for a few minutes, then after a brief rest, we exchanged "Good Lucks" and left our friend, beginning our long trudge of approximately three miles down to the lodge. Even though the rest of the way would be easy, it was in soft snow, slightly steep in places, and would take whatever reserves of energy we had left to get there.

****

A couple of hours later, we were at the lodge parking lot where I had left my pick-up truck a day earlier. We took off our boots, gaiters, wet socks, and then pulled out all of our gear and strew it around, letting the wet gear dry in the warm sun. It was fun just sitting in the sun, letting our aching feet recuperate from the many hours of weight being thrust upon them. While sorting through the gear, I picked up my helmet, and glancing at it, I realized that the force of the blow by the rock had popped out two of the rivets, which hold the webbing inside. It took quite a blow to do that.

"Bob, I think it was a good idea deciding to wear our helmets," I said as I held up my helmet and showed him the missing rivets. "I can just imagine what my head would look like if I hadn't been wearing it."

"Something that we can tell all the student climbers about," Bob replied dryly. "But on the other hand, we'd better not! Especially the homemade rope! We're supposed to set good examples you know."

A half an hour later as we were loading our gear into the truck, up walked our lone climber friend, whom we had chatted with high on the mountain.

"Hey, how are you doing? Did you get some good pictures?"

"Yeah, I got some good ones." Smiling broadly he continues, "But I have to tell you, you guys have to be two of the luckiest people I have ever met."

Bob quickly asks, "Why is that?"

The climber continues, "Just a few minutes after you headed down, I was taking some time to view the upper mountain and take pictures. I was just standing there beginning to take a picture of the snow bridge that you two had just crossed over, when it suddenly collapsed with a crash and falls into the crevasse. It scared the living heck out of me! Gosh, a few minutes earlier, and you could have been on top of it."

Bob responds, "The heck it did!"

As for me, I just smiled and nodded my head. This was a confirmation that we were truly being watched over. I knew that Bob and I were truly blessed! *I also knew that I would climb again!*

COOPER SPUR (a poem)
By
Gary Metternich

Every mountain has a route that can entice,
and lure for sure. Mt. Hood has one; a **killer**;
and it's called **Cooper Spur.**

Many have climbed it; many have paid the price, for
the Northeast ridge is calling; it is steep, and covered
with ice.

We headed out too late that morn; it was
warm, breezy, almost hot.
 On the steepest section, we heard a "crack"
high above us; like a rifle shot!

We didn't look up, for with our experience,
it was easy to know,
that rocks were cart-wheeling down upon us,
followed by snow.

Was this finally the end? Was it our time to die?
But except for a few bruises, the whole thing went
roaring by.

Heading for the summit, we knew in our mind we'd
climb again and again, only because **God** was so kind.

Footnotes:
1973- Father and son fall to their deaths while climbing the
route.

June 6, 1981- Two climbers die while descending route, David
Turple and Bill Pilkenton.

June 21, 1981- Seven climbers fall while descending the route.
Five climbers die, Jim Darby, Garth Westcott, Larry Young,
George Anderson, Leah Lorenson.

July, 1994- Four climbers fall 700 ft. while descending route.
Two die, Ole Groupe and Jerry Milton.

September, 1997- Mark Fraas dies after falling 1,500 ft. while
climbing the route.

May, 1999- Two climbers fall 1,500 ft. and die while
descending the route.

June, 2000- Diana Kornet falls 2,500 ft. down the Cooper Spur
route after reaching the summit from another route and dies.

May, 2002- Snowboarder, Juan Carlos Munoz falls 2,500 ft.
down the route while trying to snowboard the route and dies.

CHAPTER III

DOUBLE TROUBLE – PART I
MT. JEFFERSON

Sometimes in life, you have a friend or an acquaintance that seemingly every time that you venture together things go wrong. I've often seen this happen in the game of golf, where each time that you play together, both of your games go haywire. I don't believe in jinx s, but there does seem to be a jinx when bad things happen so often. So it is with three of my stories and having the one same climbing partner.

On Independence Day, the 4th of July, after having pancakes at the Polk County Fairgrounds Fireman's Breakfast, Hank and I jumped into his little Volkswagen Beetle and headed east up Highway 22, to take us to the White River Trailhead. The trailhead was located at the end of a dirt road near the Santiam Pass, southeast of Detroit, Oregon. Our destination was the north face of Mt. Jefferson, and a route named the Jeff Park Glacier.

Mt. Jefferson, at 10,495 ft. is the second highest mountain in the state of Oregon. An old volcano, it is one of many dormant volcanoes situated in the Central Cascade mountain range. It is located approximately eighty miles southeast of Salem, Oregon, and lies within a string of mountains separating western and eastern Oregon. Because of its location, the weather can be unpredictable, since it may be rainy and foul weather in the western valleys, but at the same time warm and dry in the central desert plains.

Altitude wise, it is not an impressive mountain, but because of the features of the mountain, it is considered one of the tougher climbs in Oregon. On this rugged mountain, you will find several major heavily crevassed glaciers, steep ridges consisting of ice and rotten rock, sheer faces, and a myriad of sharp pinnacles looking from afar like sentries, blocking many of the routes.

Our plan was to make this a warm up climb for another planned trip to climb Washington's Mt. Rainier ten days later. We had chosen one of the tougher routes on the mountain, with our reasoning being that it would afford us better conditioning, with possibly some technical ice climbing. We were hoping that it would also place us far away from the many 4th of July holiday hikers and climbers.

My partner on this climb was Hank Keeton. I had only met Hank the previous autumn of the year when he had called my office. I was a partner in a CPA firm in Monmouth, Oregon, that specialized in small business and income taxes. One early afternoon I received a call, which my secretary informed me was from a possible new client. After answering the phone, I heard a voice from the other end state that he had checked around, and found that I was a climber, as well as a CPA. I acknowledged with humility that indeed I was a climber. He then said, "I want you to be my CPA. When are you available to talk to me?" I informed him that I had some time open later that afternoon, and he could drop by for a "get acquainted" meeting. He agreed.

That afternoon, shortly after five o'clock, he dropped by. Meeting him in the waiting room, I introduced myself, and invited him into my office. As we walked into my office, I noticed that he was carrying a brown paper sack, which isn't unusual to see in an accounting firm. I was hoping that it was not a bunch of bills and receipts!

"Hey Boss, I brought you something!"

Curiously, I answered, "You did? That was nice of you."

He then opened the sack and pulled out a six-pack of little green bottles: ***Rainier Ale.*** "I just discovered this recently. Great stuff! Have you tried it?"

I hadn't, but I knew that I was about to. I was a little nervous about drinking beer in my office since my partner was a bishop in the Mormon Church, and really frowned on anyone drinking alcoholic beverages, as well as anything with caffeine in it. Oh well, the business day was over, and of course I didn't want to offend a possible new client, especially a fellow climber. "No I haven't, but it looks interesting," I replied.

We spent the next couple of hours drinking the ale, and talking about climbing. I realized in a short time that this person was not just another peak bagger, but someone who had spent a lot of time in the outdoors, and like me, it was an important part of his life. Hank had been raised in California, and spent much of his younger years hiking and climbing in the Sierras, a major mountain range in California. He had attended Berkeley (University of California) and recently had received his PHD. Now, he had come to Oregon to start a construction business with two other Partners. He had also bought a beautiful piece of property on the eastern side of the Willamette Valley, far away from the towns and population. It was set in the mountains, and had several small lakes on it. His plans were to someday build a beautiful house near the largest lake, but at the present had acquired a mobile home, in which he also had his office.

Hank's climbing experience was quite different from mine in that he had spent considerable time climbing rock in Yosemite, and other nearby rock climbing areas. Since he had a great barbecue pit at his home in the mountains, I spent many evenings there enjoying the good food, and talking about Yosemite and some of his old climbing friends. This was especially interesting to someone who had only climbed on the rotten rock of the North Cascades. It was here that we made our plans for a trip up Mt. Rainier. But first, a warm up climb on Mt. Jefferson.

****

The Santiam River is a beautiful little river, winding and cascading down the pass along highway 22. We could see fishermen in spots along the banks, trying to catch that one prize trout, or at least enough to take home for a worthy meal. We turned off the highway when we reached the cut-off and the sign indicating the Whitewater Creek Road. The next fifteen or so miles were on a rough, dusty dirt road, with wash boards so bad in places that it almost threw the vehicle off the road. Finally, we were at the end of the road, and at the trailhead where we would begin our hike into the base of the mountain, to what is called Jefferson Park.

After finding a suitable place among the dozen or so other vehicles also parked at the trailhead, we pulled out all of our gear, sorting it and deciding who was to carry what, and then loaded our packs. Within twenty minutes we were ready to stash our wallets, and lock up the vehicle. We then hoisted our packs to our shoulders, and began our hike.

The weather was partially cloudy but warm. The weather forecast was for "iffy" weather for the long holiday week-end, but since Mt. Jefferson seems to have its own weather due to its' location between western and central Oregon, we decided to try it anyway. Even if we were weathered off, we would at least have the conditioning of a long hike in and back with heavy packs.

The trail into Jefferson Park is probably one of the better trails in Oregon for its mild rate of ascent, and the beautiful scenery along the trail. It is a six and one half mile hike, first through deep forests of fir, pine and hemlock, then along rocky exposed trails with views down to the valley floor. Later you come to some clearings where the mountain can be seen with its steep glaciers flowing down from sharp ridges and pinnacles, with the water cascading from the glaciers to the many creeks and streams, carving their way through the mountains on the way to the ocean. The trail crosses streams and creeks with bubbling pure water running over rocks and boulders of gray granite. You may even encounter banks of firm snow left over from the fierce winter, melting slowly amidst the shade and in some places forming small pools or tarns. At last, the trees begin to thin, and you find yourself in an open area of meadows and lakes. You are on a little plateau settled below the mountain and surrounding ridges. This is Jefferson Park. It is not a man-made park as some would think, but a natural park. With its location at close to seven thousand feet in altitude, with wild flowers, patches of snow, and many small lakes of various shapes, sizes and colors, the beauty here cannot be matched. To top it off, on the south side of the park, rising steeply just beyond the trees and brush is the north face of Mt. Jefferson.

Within two hours, we had hiked the six miles and were now entering the park at the base of the mountain. After staring at the spectacular view in front of us a few minutes, we began searching for a place to set up our camp. We soon found a nice spot, nearer to the mountain, nestled in a clearing near the wild flowers, and close enough to a lake to provide our water and bathing. Satisfied that we had found the perfect location for our home for two nights, we took off our packs and began unloading them.

"I'm impressed Metternich! What scenery!"

"Hank, it is about the most beautiful spot that I know of" I replied. I looked up from what I was doing, and glancing around at the sky and clouds added, "It also looks like the weather is holding so far. I'm looking for a good climb tomorrow."

"I hope to shout!" answered Hank back. "What about our route? How does it look to you?"

Looking directly up at the steep Jeff Park Glacier, it looked to be in good condition. Since this was early July, there was plenty of snow on the mountain, and the crevasses, which normally run all the way across the glacier in later summer, seemed to be passable. From this distance, I couldn't really determine what the conditions were like higher up towards the top of the glacier. Hopefully, we wouldn't have to traverse far to our right to get around the bergschrund, the main crevasse near the top. I was hoping for a nice snow bridge to cross rather than having to climb the extremely steep slope on the right side of the glacier that hung onto the side of a ridge.

"From here, it's looking good! After going up that narrow moraine, we'll rope up, get onto the glacier, and then head up the left side. It looks pretty straight forward, and we should be able to skirt around to the left of those crevasses until we get to the bergschrund. Then we'll see if there is some way across. Our main concern going up will be possible rock fall from the cliffs on the left. You can see the stuff lying there from previous days. Once we get across the bergschrund, we'll head straight up that steep ice until we reach the ridge on the very top. You can't see the summit pinnacle from here because it is to the left, and quite a way back, behind those other pinnacles. Once gaining the ridge, we will traverse to our left, and then angle down onto steep boulders, which are quite exposed, in order to get around two of the pinnacles. If I remember correctly, you are looking straight down hundreds of feet. If traversing doesn't look good, possibly, we can climb over the top of the pinnacles, but the one previous time that I climbed this route we didn't. What do you think?"

"You're the boss. We'll know what it's like tomorrow. Bye the way, did you say that your tent was a two-man?" Hank asked.

Hank was referring to the small MSR tent that I had purchased recently on sale in Seattle, at the home of MSR. It was one of the first tents made out of Gore-Tex, and very lightweight. Even though it was described as a two-man tent, it looked like it would be crowded, even without any of our gear in it. I had purchased it with the intent to use it on Mt. Rainier, since I wanted to go as light as possible, hoping to take our packs all the way to the summit, and then descending by the standard route.

"Yep, but it might just be a little cozy," I answered.

"You don't snore do you?" asked Hank.

"Not very often," I replied.

We heated our water, and after a dinner of freeze dried food, accompanied by tea, we went about the business of getting our gear ready for a very early morning start. Our plan was to get up around midnight, and head up the mountain around one a.m. Glaciers should be traveled only under solid conditions, and with the additional concern of rock fall, we wanted to be up past the more dangerous areas before the ice and snow began to soften.

Soon we were snuggled in our sleeping bags, or a better description would be that we were crammed into our miniature tent. It was so small that neither of us could adjust our position. Aside from being very uncomfortable, I also laid there envisioning what the route might be like and our events of the next day. This is something I always do the night before a climb, and it can lessen the few hours that you have to sleep. After, my usual evening talk with God, asking for a safe climb, I settled into the world of dreams.

****

When at last the alarm went off around twelve midnight, I found myself relieved to finally be getting out of that uncomfortable tent, and stretching my body. As usual, I would just have to ignore the little bit of sleep I had during the night, and push my body as if I had a full night's rest. I found through experience that the flow of adrenaline combined with the pure air could make up for a lack of sleep, at least for one night. Hank had not done much better, and he grumbled about me keeping him awake with my snoring. I denied it of course, but it was a confirmation to me that I had caught a couple of "winks."

At one thirty a.m. we put on our packs, grabbed our ice axes, and with our head lamps turned on began heading up the path leading to the edge of the trees. We headed up through the brush, and then onto the snow next to the rocky moraine. The snow was quite firm, making it difficult kicking steps, but it was easier than slipping and sliding up the sandy and rocky moraine. Soon however, the snow became too steep and since we didn't have our crampons on, we angled over to the moraine. We grunted our way up the soft dirt and rock on the side of the moraine, sometimes sliding back a foot or two, until we reached the narrow top of it, which we then proceeded to follow. The footing from here was still soft and rocky, and it took a lot of effort and energy to hike the moraine up to the edge of the glacier.

An hour or so later, we were at the edge of the glacier, where we dropped our packs and began our rest break among the boulders. The sky was black and a few stars were shining through the clouds. There was a slight breeze blowing, and we began to get chilled since our bodies were damp from the sweat we had produced while moving up the steep moraine, so we put on our parkas to stay warm. After having some water and snacks, we huddled down among the rocks, waiting for the first signs of the light of dawn before we would begin our next climbing up the steep glacier.

I half dozed as I sat there. I thought about how nice it would be, lying in a warm bed, with my head on a soft pillow. Soon, we would be moving up the steep glacier, and our bodies would rebel against the exertion in the middle of the night. The first half an hour is especially difficult after a long break, since the muscles become stiff, and the lungs do not want to cooperate. What kind of sport was it that demanded so much out of the human body in the middle of the night? Did I really love doing this, or was I a little crazy? Surely, there must be some other kind of recreation that gave me the same satisfaction, but required much less effort. These same thoughts were with me each time I ventured out to climb another mountain. And then, there was the risk! You try not to think about it, but in the back of your mind there is always the thought that a loose rock falling from high above you, a slip on the steep ice by you or your climbing partner, or the collapse of a snow bridge over a hidden crevasse might end your life that day. Was it really worth it, trying to reach the summit of a mountain? Maybe you should be with the family having breakfast together in the morning, then an afternoon in the park. Or possibly, playing eighteen holes of golf with your friends, then going to the clubhouse and having a couple of beers and discussing your golf game. Was this that you were doing a mostly selfish thing, something being shared with only one friend? I knew at this moment of time, and at this place, this question could not be answered. Instead, I would need to turn my attention to what lie ahead, and concentrate on using my skills to insure a safe and successful climb.

With the very first sign of light on the glacier, we got up, stretched our stiff bodies, and then went about the business of putting on our crampons. The crampons, which are steel spike-like attachments that go under the boots, were icy cold, and working with them made my fingers ache from the cold. Soon, they were firmly attached, and I put my hands back into my warm gloves. Next, I grabbed the rope and uncoiled it, carefully laying it on the glacier ice. Since it was 120 feet long, I doubled it so that Hank and I would be sixty feet apart. I then tied a figure eight knot, and hooked the carabiner attached to my harness through the loop. I attached the two prussik slings to the rope, clipping the end of the short one into my harness. Prussiks are small rope slings which can be used in emergency, like hanging in a crevasse, to work your way up and out, by alternately sliding the ropes up, and at the same time moving your hands and legs up. Putting pressure on the prussik rope causes the knot to tighten on the climbing rope, allowing the individual to stand in one loop or to sit hanging from the other loop. This is a very strenuous and difficult procedure, and one that I hoped I would never need to use.

Once we were both properly attached to the climbing rope, I turned and asked Hank, "Are you ready to rock?"

"Let's roll, boss!" came the reply.

I headed up the left side of the glacier, trying to avoid the rocks of many sizes, which had fallen in the past few days from the rock pinnacles higher up. Hank waited, and as soon as the slack of the rope was taken up between us, he followed.

The glacier on this side was practically free of crevasses except for small fissures which we easily stepped over. The Jefferson Park glacier becomes steep quickly, and soon we were kicking in our crampons hard to make sure that we had good footing. The ice was too hard at this point to kick steps, so we had to rely solely on our cramponing abilities. It was getting lighter with each few minutes, but it would still be a few hours before the sun, which was rising to the east of us, would peer over the rocky ridge and pinnacles and give us warmth.

The visibility ahead was good, and I could make out what seemed to be larger crevasses crossing horizontally directly above us a few hundred feet. There also seemed to be some crevasses running parallel to the direction we were traveling. It is at this point that route finding becomes interesting. Hopefully, I could find a somewhat direct route through, avoiding having to backtrack, looking for alternatives and losing precious time. In addition to this, I wanted to show Hank that I was competent in my leading abilities.

Up to this point, the weather seemed a little muggy, but some stars were still showing and I did not see warnings of any kind of storm coming in. Daylight would give us much better indications of what the weather would be like.

I approached the large crevasse first, which ran parallel to us. I continued along it, but just close enough to be able to see in it, and follow the line ahead with my eyes to make sure that it did not turn and hollow out underneath us. Ahead, probably less than a rope length was a very large crevasse. This one ran horizontal to the steep slope. As I approached it, I could see that there were no snow bridges available to cross, and the crevasse was too wide to jump. We would have to go around. Since the parallel crevasse that we had been walking along side of nearly extended to the one above, I decided to turn to the right and follow the crevasse lying ahead of us along its shoulder, and look for a place to skirt around the end. Approximately one hundred feet later I was at the end of the crevasse, and then veered around it, giving myself plenty of spare room just in case it was hollow underneath.

In another hour we had zigzagged our way up and around the major crevasses, and were heading for the big one, the bergschrund. The bergschrund is normally the final crevasse that separates the glacier from the mountain beneath it. It can be enormous, with the upper lip ten to twenty feet high. Quite impassable! Other times, there will be a snow bridge across to the upper lip. On some occasions, you can skirt around the end of the crevasse, climbing through broken ice and gaining the mountain's rock. On other occasions you climb down into the crevasse a short ways, finding a snow bridge to the other side, then do some ice climbing to gain the upper top of the lip. We were in luck! There seemed to be a snow bridge near the left end of the crevasse, close to the rocks. I headed there. Much to my delight, it was a good crossing. After having Hank put me on belay, I was soon across and then belayed Hank over.

Next we headed up the extreme steep upper portion above the crevasse. This was a place that you didn't want to slip, because a fall from here into the crevasse below would be certain death.

"Hank, the ice seems to be perfect for a little front-pointing, and the angle is not too steep, so I don't think that I need to place an ice screw. Do you want me to place any protection?"

I thought I knew what Hank's answer would be, since he had told me of some of his harrowing climbing experiences in Yosemite. "No, let's just go for it!" he shouted back.

"Right on! It's only a short distance and we'll be off this hard ice and climbing on less steep snow" I added.

Soon we were in softer snow and I was able to kick good steps all the way up to the top where the ridge was. Approaching the ridge, I realized that there was no rock showing as there was in my past climb of this route. The whole mountain, except for a few patches on the very steep pitches on the cliffs to my left was covered in dazzling white ice. What a beautiful site this was. From the top of the ridge, which was more like a large saddle between towering pinnacles, I could see the main summit pinnacle shining in the background. It was still a quarter of mile away. Ahead of us was probably the crux of the entire climb, getting beyond the two pinnacles on my left, which were blocking our path along this ridge. On my previous climb of this route, we had climbed down twenty to thirty feet to a ledge system; from there we traversed around the two pinnacles. From where I now stood, a ledge system did not exist! It was a sheer, icy drop off of several hundred feet to the Milk Creek Glacier below.

I coiled the rope and laid it down at my feet as Hank kicked his way to the top. Since he had never climbed this mountain before, I watched him closely to see the expression on his face as he eyed the surroundings before him. As he approached where I was standing, he looked around, surveying every bit of the terrain, his eyes searching out the same thing that I had looked for, a way to the summit pinnacle.

"Where do we go from here, Boss?"

"Well Hank, under normal conditions, towards the end of this saddle, just before that first pinnacle, you traverse down the boulders until you come to a ledge. Then you follow that ledge, traversing around both pinnacles, then climb back up to the ridge, and follow it over to the summit pinnacle. The problem is, the route is covered with ice, and very exposed." Thinking back on my previous climb of this route, I added, "I'm not sure that even if we didn't have all this snow, the traverse would work."

"Why is that, partner?"

"When we climbed this a few years ago, and as we were traversing down there around the first pinnacle, the rocks broke loose between Bob True and me, and took a great portion of the ledge system with it. It happened a few feet ahead of me. I thought for sure that we had lost Bob. Then as the dust settled, I heard Bob yell that he was okay. Apparently the rocks between us dropped straight down to the glacier below. Man! What a scary thing! If we had been roped, we would have both gone. It makes my knees shake just thinking about it. Anyway, it looks like we find another way around, or head home. The ridge behind us drops down to the Russell Glacier, which is an easier route than the one we just came up, just in case we need to head down."

"What about climbing over those pinnacles?" questioned Hank.

"We can go take a look. It looks pretty hairy though!" I replied with some degree of hesitation. To me it looked very questionable, but the thought of turning back didn't appeal to me either.

Still roped, we headed along the ridge towards the first pinnacle. Approaching the pinnacle, I could see that it was completely encrusted in ice. The height of the pinnacle wasn't over fifteen feet, but the exposure on each side was enough to make you want to turn back. As I drew closer, the ridge narrowed significantly, leaving only one direction to go, and that was onto the pinnacle itself. Even more alarming, was the condition of the ice on the pinnacle. It was wind-blown, and the melting and re-freezing created an icicle type texture, with hollow areas beneath. I had a knot in my stomach from just looking at it. I really couldn't see how we would be able to get any kind of secure grip with our ice axe and crampons. It looked to me like any attempt would result in a breaking off of the ice and subsequently a fall. Even though we would be roped, at nine thousand feet in altitude, this was no place to end up being injured.

"Hank, I don't like the looks of this ice at all! I don't think we can get a decent bite with our ice axes." At this point, I thought that we would be heading back.

"Hell, let me give it a try!" was the surprising reply from Hank.

"Well, I don't think I really care to. If you're willing, move up here and I'll put you on belay."

Hank moved up to where I was standing, all the time eyeing the exposed move in front of him. I knelt down, driving my ice axe as deep as I could into the snow, then wound the rope around the axe in order to hold a possible fall. As soon as the rope was taut, Hank moved up to the pinnacle. He then raised his ice axe and tried thrusting it into the ice on the pinnacle. Chunks of ice broke off as the ice axe found only hollowness beneath. He tried again. Still, the ice axe could not be planted firmly in the ice. Trying a third time, the ice axe held, but looked questionable. He then said, "I'm going to try it!"

He then kicked in his boot, trying to get a hold with his crampons. More ice broke off and fell to the glacier below. Again and again he kicked in his boot, finally securing a foothold. He pulled his body up, kicked in his other foot, and then hugged the pinnacle. While grasping the ice with his left hand and placing all his weight on his crampons, he then pulled the ice axe free, moving it further around the pinnacle, and tried jamming it into the ice. Again, chunks of ice broke off. He tried again, finally getting a bite, and then carefully freed one foot, and kicked it into the ice further around the corner. He continued these series of movements until he had disappeared around the corner of the pinnacle.

The rope stopped running through my hands, and I heard him yell back "O.K., you can take me off belay. I am in a position to belay you around, so let me know when you're ready."

I don't know if I will ever be ready, I thought. "Go ahead and take up the rope," I called to Hank. The slack rope began moving in Hank's direction. Suddenly, to my amazement, I heard voices behind me. What the heck! I quickly turned my head, and quite a distance back of me, where we had first gained the ridge I saw a climber come into view, but from the other side where the Russell Glacier route tops out. "Hank, I think we have company. Looks like another climbing party behind us."

"I'm ready for you. I have you on belay!" Hank yelled back. The rope was now taut between us.

I immediately forgot about the other climbers, and looked ahead at the scary task ahead of me. I could feel the nervousness in my body, and the knot that had formed in my stomach as I responded to Hank, "Climbing!" I thought, *here goes nothing*!

I tried following Hank's moves, first with my ice axe. I just couldn't seem to get it to bite. Each time that I tried jamming it into the ice, chunks would fall off. I was about ready to give up, but I thought, *I have to get over to Hank! I have no choice!* Finally, the pick on my axe stuck. I didn't dare test it, as it might pull out. I then leaned toward the icy pinnacle, and began kicking in my left boot. Again, chunks of ice broke off and fell through the space below me. My legs were beginning to shake! I certainly didn't need that now! I kicked again very hard, breaking through the remaining icicles and found some solid ice beneath. This would have to do. I carefully put my weight on it, then swung my other leg up and began kicking into the ice. The exposure below me was terrifying! Even though Hank had me on belay, it was frightening and I was prepared to peel off at any moment. I wasn't sure how secure Hank was in his position since I couldn't see him around the corner. If I fell, there was the possibility that I could pull him off his stance, and we would both fall. The sweat was beginning to run down into my eyes now, even though the temperature was cold. It was taking great effort to climb around this pinnacle requiring my full concentration on each little movement. Soon, I was working on my next move, which didn't seem quite so bad. Whew! At last, I had turned the corner, and could now see Hank.

"**Holy Moly!** That was incredible!" I exclaimed between gasping breaths.

"We did it partner!" Hank replied, as he continued to belay me.

"You freakin did it, Hank!" That was an incredibly daring piece of ice work back there! I couldn't find a solid hold on that whole pinnacle. Matter of fact, I really felt that I was going to fall off a couple of times!"

"I did too, Boss! What's that other climbing party doing back there anyway?" asked Hank.

"I'm not sure. They seem to be lost or something. I have a feeling that they were watching me, and probably decided to turn around after seeing what we had to do. It was really unnerving having them watch me." Then, looking towards the next pinnacle, I continued "Looks like the rest of this is not too bad. Keep me on belay, and I'll just go around you, then continue on."

We were on a small saddle between the two pinnacles, and it looked like it would be easy to skirt around the next one. I moved forward, and soon was working my way around the next pinnacle. Once I was around it and back again on the ridge, I drove my ice axe into the snow, and told Hank who was approximately forty feet behind that he could climb. As I was belaying Hank, I noticed that some clouds had drifted in, and it looked like that we would soon be enveloped in them. The sky above had also turned from blue to gray, and I sensed that we were in for a change of weather. The summit pinnacle was still another half an hour or more away, and I hoped that we could get over there, climb to the summit, and get down before any major change in the weather occurred.

Within a few minutes Hank had joined me, and as we looked at the summit pinnacle, we discussed the options available to us. I had planned on descending the "standard" route after summiting, which would be going in the opposite direction of where we were. Even though that descent route involved a very steep traverse of a couple of hundred feet across, just south of the pinnacle, the rest of the way was not too difficult. It did require down climbing a steep ridge to the White Water Glacier, then navigating through the heavily crevassed glacier. It wouldn't be easy, but at least I was familiar with the route. I had never been down this west side of the mountain, with its steep Milk Creek glaciers. The key, we agreed, was getting up the summit as soon as possible, and beating any kind of storm. If we did in fact get into a bad storm, then we would have the option of back tracking, then climbing down the Milk Creek glacier next to the route that we had just come up, to a point where we could traverse over and join the Russell Creek glacier route, being the one that the other party had just come up. In no way would we go back across the pinnacles that we had just climbed!

Keeping the rope spread out between us, we quickly headed east along the ridge, which then curved south and towards the summit. The going was safe, with the ridge top being ten to fifteen feet wide in most places. We had to negotiate one more pinnacle in the middle of the ridge, climbing up and over it, but soon we were back on the ridge again. As we approached the main summit pinnacle, I glanced back along our route, and thought I could see the other climbers rappelling off the ridge, down to the Milk Creek glacier. What were they doing? Why didn't they just retrace their tracks back down the Russell route? Soon, the clouds drifted in, and I lost sight of them.

The summit pinnacle is over two hundred feet high. It looks impressive, but if you know where you are going, it is merely a careful scramble up a ledge system of loose rocks to the top. However, if you don't know what you're doing, any other way up could be dangerous, with some technical climbing involved. I was thinking that I could easily find the route, but then the clouds began to obscure my view of the pinnacle. Within minutes we were in a white out, and barely able to see two yards ahead of us. Before the clouds had drifted in, I was able to focus in on what I thought to be the beginning of the route up the pinnacle, so I continued to head in that general direction.

As I came to the place that I felt we should start climbing up the pinnacle, I yelled back at Hank and told him that I was going to coil in the rope so we would be closer together. Soon he was right behind me.

"The snow is pretty soft here, so I think we'll just stay close together in this white out and see how far we can get up this pinnacle. If it gets too icy, then we'll have to belay one another."

As we began heading up, I thought about how nice it would be if the clouds would blow off now and then, so that I could get a view of the pinnacle and make sure where we were headed. Slowly we cramponed our way up, all the while making sure that we had a good bite with each stroke of our ice axes. The route as I remembered it did not go straight up, but zig-zagged around some major boulders. It looked so different to me now, being covered with ice. We continued to work our way up; fifty feet; a hundred feet; then one hundred fifty feet. I knew that we were getting close to the summit, but darn, I couldn't see a thing! I was moving slowly now, being very cautious, as I remembered the awesome drop-off on my right, that I was probably very close to now. Finally, I came to a spot that I guessed was the summit boulder. At this point the snow had become icy, and the footing increasingly difficult. The rocks were covered with ice, and impossible to grasp hold of.

I waited for Hank, and as soon as he had caught up with me, I said, "Hank, I think that this is as far as we can go. We top out just around that little corner, and then just a few feet higher. But, there is nothing but thin air around that corner, and we would have to crawl over those ice-covered rocks. So my friend, I'm calling this the summit! Climbers hate not having touched the very top. "I'll tell you one fact that you will appreciate, no one has summited this mountain before us this year!"

"Sounds alright to me. No sense chancing a fall just to touch the very top. You can't see a damn thing anyway!" answered Hank approvingly.

"I was hoping that this soup was going to clear away, but apparently it isn't, so our next decision will be how to get down off this mountain. First, let's get off this pinnacle, then maybe we'll head over to where I believe the steep traverse begins down the standard route, and we'll make a decision there. Hopefully I can find the darn thing!"

Hank asked, "What about the Milk Creek Glacier, just below where we came around that ridge? Isn't that an option that we discussed?"

"You're right. That is our other option, but what I know is that it's very steep, and I've never been down it before. I don't even know if it's crevassed or not, and not being able to see down it is a little frightening. Possibly, we could go down it a ways, and try to cross over to the Russell route around the 9,500 ft. level. I have my altimeter, so I could keep an eye on it as we descend." After pondering this a minute, I added, "Let's see what the standard route is like first."

"You're the boss. I'll follow you." Hank added, "at least we have options."

Sometimes, it is nicer not being the "boss." Somehow, over the years, I seemed to find myself in that situation. Even in the Marine Corps., I sometimes had unwanted responsibility thrown upon me. It is easier following others, but I have to admit, the personal rewards are greater being the leader if you are successful. The key, "successful."

We retraced our tracks down the steep pinnacle, being extra careful that we didn't slip since we still had our rope in coils between us. It didn't take long before we were at the bottom of the pinnacle. I headed to the left, and began traversing below the summit pinnacle. I knew that I had at least a rope length to go before I came to the area where the traverse would become extremely steep. The white out had become increasingly worse, and I could barely see anything in front of me now. I had removed my climbing goggles quite a while ago, hoping to see better, but even this wasn't doing any good now.

After carefully traversing along the bottom of the pinnacle a hundred feet or more, and then walking along what seemed a bulge in the snow, I suddenly came to a bottomless void in front of me. I seemed to have come abruptly to the edge of the snow, and it appeared that there was a drop off after a few more inches into space. Was this the beginning of the steep traverse? If so, it was scary! Had my route taken me too high? Or possible, did I go too low? Damn! If I could just see ahead of me! Why won't this stuff just clear up for a few seconds, giving me the opportunity to find the way across? I waited. Hank, having sensed that I had stopped, also came to a halt, keeping the rope taut.

"Hey boss, what do you see?" Hank asked.

I replied, with frustration in my voice, "I can't see a damn thing! It looks awfully steep though, and I don't think I can go any further. Either I am in the wrong place, or the terrain has changed a lot since I was last here."

I waited, hoping to get a glimpse of what lay ahead, and at the same time, trying to think of the alternatives. The snow was too soft to put protection in. I knew trying to go ahead without protection would be foolish. This traverse was the crux of the climb on most of the routes on this mountain. Normally it is very steep, and even under good conditions requires the utmost of care getting across. Like all things on a mountain, its conditions change, and sometimes can be almost impassable. It is so steep that if you slip here, the hopes of self-arrest are almost impossible, with the result being a fall of a few thousand feet and certain death. More than one person in past years had done exactly that. I felt that we really didn't have any choice but to turn around, and try to find a way down the Milk Creek glacier.

"Hank, we need to turn back! Let's trace our tracks back under the pinnacle to the ridge, then we'll try to find some way down from there."

"Got you boss!" Hank probably knew that we were dead-ended. He turned around, and began heading in the direction where we came.

We could make out our tracks in the soft ice, and slowly, carefully, retraced them past the pinnacle to the ridge. Once we were on less steep ice, I called out to Hank to stop, and wait for me to traverse over to where he was.

Coming up beside him, I exclaimed, "That was pretty darn hairy back there! It dropped straight down, and I couldn't see a thing ahead of me. I wasn't about to take another step. I really had hoped that I could find some way to traverse that section, but it just won't clear up."

"This white out is a bad one! Hopefully we don't have to dig ourselves in, and wait it out," responded Hank.

"I think we can get down, but it might be real slow, since it's pretty darn steep! Also, I'm not sure of what will be below us. Hopefully no crevasses! Why don't I lead out, following the ridge for a while, then I'll angle down the snow near where the ridge curves, where it's not quite so steep?" If it gets too steep, then we'll have to belay, but since the snow is so soft, we may not have to. Okay partner?"

"Yep, let's give it a try!" came Hanks reply.

As I headed along the ridge, I stepped into our tracks we had made coming up. It felt good to see human tracks, even though they were ours, and knowing that we couldn't follow them all the way in descending the mountain. After traversing a couple of hundred feet along the ridge, I started angling down onto the glacier. The snow was soft, the footing good, and it was less steep here than below the area where we had just traversed. The snow was beginning to ball up under my crampons and occasionally I would lift my foot and hit my crampons with my ice axe to knock the accumulated snow off. It was easy to slip and fall when the snow was balled up under your crampons.

I tried to stay close to the ridge on my way down, because I knew that eventually we would want to cross over to it. The problem was that I couldn't see it! It wasn't long before the angle began getting steeper. I wasn't sure how steep it would get, but I recalled that on my previous climb, I had looked down at this section, and it seemed to be reasonable, possibly forty-five, or at the most fifty degrees.

I was trying to be very careful with the placement of my steps, kicking in my heels as much as possible, and every few steps knocking the balled up snow from underneath my crampons. Looking down into the gray gave me an uneasy feeling, like I might possible step off a cliff at any moment, but I kept moving down slowly.

Suddenly Hank yelled out "falling!" His feet had slipped from underneath him, and he began sliding down the slope. I didn't even turn to look at him, but instantly went into self-arrest, falling on my stomach, and digging the ice axe into the snow. Hank was trying to go into arrest also, but because of the steep soft snow, went sliding down past me. I kicked in the toes of my boots, waiting for the tug on the rope. As he hit the end of the rope, I felt the hard tug on my waist, with the force pushing my toes even deeper into the snow. He stopped! The arrest had worked!

"Hank, are you okay?"

"Yep, I'm fine. My crampons kept balling up under me, and it was like being on roller skates!"

"I'll slow it down a little, so we will have time to knock that stuff off our crampons as we move," I responded.

We both got slowly up on our feet, and I slowly went down around him, and began descending again. We hadn't down climbed another five minutes when Hank called out again! I again fell down into self-arrest, and he went sailing past me. Again the tug, and then he stopped.

"This stuff is bull shit!" Hank said disgustedly. "I can't seem to get any good footing at all!"

I knew that Hank was embarrassed by his falling. "I know what you mean Hank. I've nearly fallen several times. If only this stuff would clear up so we could see what is below us." Looking at my altimeter, I added, "I believe we still have a ways to go before we can traverse over. Probably another thousand feet." I was straining my eyes to see below me, but to no avail. "Dear Lord, I really need your help right now. Just clear it up for a moment, so I can get my bearing, and see what is below me," I quietly prayed. I continued to stand there, looking at the gray white all around me. Even though we were in a whiteout, there wasn't much of a breeze, and my body was wet with perspiration. I was also beginning to feel the fatigue setting in, since it was around noon, and we had been climbing for over eleven hours with only one major rest break.

I was about to take my next step down, when suddenly it began clearing below me. Within seconds, it had cleared sufficiently enough that I could see far down the glacier, and what I saw made my heart jump. It looked like a clear run out all the way down a snowfield. Apparently we had traversed over to a snowfield rather than going down the main part of the Milk Creek glacier. What's more, it seemed to be free of crevasses below, although still steep. The clearing lasted just a few seconds, but it gave me a clear picture of what lay before us. "Thank you Lord for the help!" This was an answer to my prayer.

"Hank, did you get a view of that?

"I sure did, boss!" came his quick reply.

"It looks good below. I think we have it made now! Matter of fact, why don't we try a controlled glissade down this, since we'll probably be falling and sliding anyway?"

"Seems like an excellent idea to me! Probably should remove our crampons though," Hank pointed out.

If the points of the crampons get caught during a glissade, you can easily break a leg, or even possibly go tumbling end over end. "You're right," I acknowledged, knowing that glissading or sliding with crampons could be dangerous. "Let's take them off here, and then we'll head down. Let's stay roped though just in case there could be some hidden crevasse in our path."

We planted our ice axes deeply into the snow, and went about the task of removing the crampons from our boots, and then attaching them to our packs. As soon as we were done, we got down into our glissade positions, spreading our legs slightly and using the ice axe like a boat rudder, and began our sliding technique down the steep snowfield. I kept the heels of my boots dug into the snow as I began my slide, making sure not to gain too much speed and lose control. I could feel the tug of the rope as it became snug, and I began pulling Hank who was sixty feet up behind me. We both let out "hoots and hollers" as we effortlessly slid down the mountain, gaining speed quickly. What a joyous feeling, being as little kids, sliding at near neck breaking speed on our rumps, and letting the whole wilderness know about it with our yells. Most experienced mountaineers will take advantage of any chance to glissade. It is not only a lot of fun, but also saves valuable time, as well as wear and tear on the body resulting from down climbing.

One thing about having fun, it is easy to forget about important things such as how much altitude you are losing at such a fast speed. When I finally realized that I needed to get my bearing, we had descended quite a distance. I rolled over, planting the ice axe into the snow, which slowed me to a stop. I then got up on my knees, and grabbed the altimeter, which was hanging from my neck and looked to see exactly where we were. "Whoops!" In a short time we had descended further than I had expected, possibly by five hundred to a thousand feet. I couldn't be sure, because the altimeter hadn't had time to react to our quick descent.

"Hank, we may have gone too low. We probably need to start traversing over from here and see if we can find the Russell glacier. I know that if we find it, I can find the rest of the way back to our north side camp."

"How low are we, can you tell?" Hank asked.

"I would guess that we are around seven thousand five hundred. Possibly lower," I answered back. "It looks like it is finally clearing up, at least down here, so as soon as we find a ridge or some other prominent feature, I'll pull out my map and try to figure it out." Just then, I could make out what seemed to be a ridge in the direction that we would be traversing. I felt confident that the Russell glacier would be just on the other side. I anxiously called to Hank, "Let's get over to that ridge and see what we can see."

Excited, I moved out at a quick pace. It still took about twenty minutes to reach the point that I had seen. As we plodded up the dirt and rock, I tried to hurry, even more anxious to see the glacier on the other side. I was almost pulling Hank on the other end of the rope. As I gained the top of the dirt and rock and could see over the other side, I became quickly disappointed. All I could see was more snow, and what looked like another ridge at least another half an hour away.

"Looks like we're not there yet," I told Hank as I pulled up the rope between us. "We still have a ways to go, but I'm sure it must be over that next ridge. Let's undo, coil the rope and carry it, since we probably won't need it for a while."

"I don't know about you, but I could take a little break, and get some water and food in me," Hank suggested.

I agreed, beginning to feel the fatigue setting in even more. It had been many hours since we last ate. After coiling the rope, we sat down and began nibbling on the sandwiches, and other items of food that we had so far not touched on this long day. The mountain below was clear now, and we could see the immense forests below in all directions. No roads, trails or rivers, but just trees.

Removing the crampons from my boots had relieved my feet from the cold hard metal, and they began to ache, just from being on them for so many hours. I knew that once the break was over, it would be painful to get back up on them, and that the rest of my body would be rebelling against further abuse also.

After a nice long break, we struggled to our feet again, putting our packs back on, and headed out at a much slower pace for the next ridge. I began thinking about how nice our camp would be once we reached it. A good cup of coffee would really hit the spot! Then just laying around, talking about the climb, or possibly even soaking our feet in some nice cold lake to ease the pain.

As we finished crossing the snow, and began walking up the dirt and rock, I could again see in the distance what appeared to be another ridge. How could it be? I knew that the lower on the mountain you go, the larger the circumference, but where did all these little ridges fit into the scheme of things? Exasperated, I finally stopped, and pulled out my map, trying to figure out where we were. I could not find any of these little ridges on the map, but I did calculate that we should not be too far from the Russell glacier. Unless of course, that snow field that we had slid down had veered to the south, rather than straight down and due west.

I knew that we were both becoming very tired, since the both of us became very quiet. What's more, we were beginning to get thirsty, and both had only a few sips of our water remaining. "Hank, you are going to hate me telling you this, but we *ain't* there yet! It has to be close though."

"I sure hope you are right. I am getting bushed!"

Since we were out of water, I suggested that we not take another break, but keep moving. Possibly we would run into some water along the way. We kept moving, although our pace had slowed down considerably.

In the next hour or so, we had crossed three more snow slopes, and potential ridges, but still no Russell glacier. I was beginning to wonder if I was on the right mountain or not, when we came up and over the sixth ridge. There, suddenly below me was the Russell glacier! Hot dog! It was beautiful, and a lot bigger than I had expected. We had come onto the lower southern end of it, and still quite a way from the north side of the mountain.

"There it is at last! We still have quite a ways to go, since we need to cross the glacier about two thirds of the way down, just beyond that buttress on the other side."

"Looks like there is water close to the terminus of the glacier," Hank commented. "But if we descend that far, we'll have to do some climbing up to get back to where you pointed out our route to be."

"Boy, I am so darn thirsty! I think it would be worth it, just to fill up on water," I responded. In fact I was so thirsty, that it seemed that water was the only thing that mattered at that moment. "Let's go for the water. It'll give us more energy to climb over that ridge to the other side, and if we have to bivouac for the night, at least we will have water."

Without any further discussion, but now motivated by the sight of water, we headed down the moraine and soon were alongside the glacier. After plodding along on the soft scree a couple of hundred yards, we stopped. We were now nearly exhausted, probably more from dehydration than anything. I had stopped sweating hours ago, and my legs were beginning to feel like rubber. My throat also was raw from the lack of water, and the heavy breathing. The glacier looked to be in good condition, with very few crevasses, especially on our side of it. The crevasses that you could see looked very passable. The angle of the glacier was fairly steep all the way down to the area of the water, and it looked to me like we could glissade down it, saving time, and the little energy that we had left.

"Hank, what do you think about roping up, and glissading down this? It'll save us lots of time."

"The glacier looks good. I'm for it!" came Hank's reply.

We quickly uncoiled the rope, and attached ourselves to each end. Then we walked out onto the glacier, and headed down to a point that was steep enough to begin our controlled slide. Within minutes we were speedily descending the glacier on our rumps. I was again in the lead, and made sure that I kept a wary eye out for any hidden crevasses. Down and down we slid, with the cool breeze of the glacier blowing in our faces. What probably would have taken us an hour or so to descend, only took about ten to fifteen minutes. Soon, we were opposite of where the water was cascading off the glacier and down the mountain. You could now hear the roar of the water, and the sound of it was like music to our ears.

We carefully crossed the glacier, and found a point on the other side near enough to the water to fill our water bottles. If you have ever been in the wilderness, and extremely thirsty, you will know that nothing compares to satisfying that thirst with fresh ice-cold mountain water. This water was coming directly from the glacier, and was the next thing to ice. We drank it down as quickly as our throats could tolerate the coldness. I could feel the energy return to my body as I re-hydrated. I literally gulped down two liters, then sat down with my third, slowing down, and taking time to enjoy each sip. We sat in the warm sun, exhausted, but now much more motivated. I glanced back up the glacier, and was amazed that we had descended that distance in such a short time. Now, we would have to get onto the rocky moraine next to us, and climb up approximately three hundred feet, crossing over the ridge to the Jefferson Park glacier, where we had been so early in the wee hours of the morning. From there we would descend down the same moraine that we came up in the dark, then onto the snow, back through the trees and brush, and finally into Jefferson Park and our camp. There was still considerable distance to go, but nothing would halt us now, and our evening would be spent in camp, enjoying our food, and talking about what a tremendous climb we had just completed.

We arrived back in camp around six thirty that evening, a little over seventeen hours after heading out in the morning. After soaking our aching feet in the nearest lake, we ate the rest of our freeze dried dinners, finishing it off with cookies, candy and a fine cup of Lipton's tea. Hank celebrated by pulling out his little bong and having a couple of relaxing puffs.

****

The next morning, after another cramped night in the miniature tent, we packed up our gear, said good-bye to the beautiful park, and hiked the six miles back to the trail- head and our vehicle. The story does not end there! While we were gone, someone had broken into all the vehicles at the trailhead, stealing money from wallets, and then tossing the wallets over the bank into the brush. Several hikers were searching around and over the bank. Wallets, credit cards, etc. were strewn everywhere. Fortunately, Hank had put our wallets in a secure place, and the thieves even though they had broken into the car, didn't find them. Nor did they find the ice cold Rainier Ale, left in a small cooler, and hidden as well. *We found both!*

CHAPTER IV

DOUBLE TROUBLE – PART II
MT. RAINIER

After the testy experience two weeks before on Mt. Jefferson with my new climbing partner, Hank, I was looking forward to a climb with a little less drama. I knew all too well that Mt. Rainier, especially if you are off the standard route, can give you everything that you can handle. Even then, I was hoping for an exciting, yet uneventful experience that would allow us to reach the summit safely, and still have great memories.

As you approach the park's west entrance, there is a large sign across the road that reads "Mount Rainier National Park." Beyond this sign there are check-in stations operated by Federal Park employees. Upon paying the required entrance fee, in return you receive a map of the park, and other brochures of interest, including schedules of park events put on for the tourists. As you drive away from the check-in area, you become aware that you have entered a different world from which you came. Immediately before and around you are giant fir trees, and the darkness of a great forest, teeming with wildlife. As you wind your way up the narrow paved road, rays of sunlight penetrate through the trees, providing warmth to an otherwise cool and damp environment. Further along the road you get your first view of a white rushing river, ice-cold, and full of silt, flowing directly from a great glacier of the mountain, beginning its journey through the mountains, hills and valleys to the ocean.

Depending on the time of day, you may also encounter deer foraging for food along the road. If you're lucky, you might even come upon a group of stopped vehicles, with the tourists watching a black bear filling up on wild berries, seemingly oblivious to the gawking crowd. As you continue up the ever-steepening road, waterfalls of various sizes come into view, flowing over and carving their way through moss-covered rock, eventually joining the rushing river. You pass trailheads leading to scenic spots with names like "Comet Falls Trailhead", "Christine Falls," and "Indian Henry's." At these trailheads you may see many parked cars, indicating that hikers are coming and going, some on short day trips and others on more vigorous overnighters. Along the road, neatly nestled in the trees are day parks, for those just wanting to spend a few hours in the wilderness, enjoying a picnic on the provided tables and benches made from decade's old hewn logs.

As you gain elevation, you slowly emerge out of the trees, and follow the road higher and higher, close to man-made rock walls, also built decades ago, there to prevent you from driving over the steep edges, which in many places drop off hundreds of feet down the outer side of the road. You marvel at the strength and ingenuity of man of an earlier time, in building such roads. Sometimes the roads had to be carved out of solid rock, using primitive equipment along with dynamite, and often under adverse weather conditions commonly encountered in the high mountains.

Why was this effort of so many man-hours and dollars spent in putting a road high up into this wilderness? A short time later, this question in your mind is clearly answered. As you make your way around another bend in the road, you can glance up to your left, and there, to your amazement, is the largest mountain that you probably have ever seen. It is close! Oh, so close! You pull off the road and park as soon as you find an available spot. Your heart is pounding from the excitement! Quickly getting out of the car, you look up, taking in the overall view of this majestic mountain with its many glaciers, rocky buttresses and ice cliffs. If you're fortunate, and the mountain is not covered with fog or a cloud cap, which it is so much of the year, you can follow with your eyes a glacier, an enormous river of ice, up and up, until it reaches close to the top of one of the mountain's three summits. This mountain is mammoth, and it seems so close that you feel as if you can reach out and touch it, even though it is several miles away. Even from this distance, you can sometimes hear the crashing of the ice and rock plunging down the steep faces, caused by the sun's warming of ice and the loosening of the rock. The magnitude of this mountain is unimaginable, and you just stare at it in pure amazement. You don't want to leave this spot, this place in time. **This is Mount Rainier.**

As a mountain, Rainier has no peers in the contiguous United States of America. Of all the mountains in North America, only Mt. McKinley in Alaska is larger, and has more glacial ice. Mt. Rainier at a height of 14,411 ft. is a giant compared to the other mountains of the Cascade Range, which runs from Canada in the north through Washington, Oregon and into California. Even the giant Mt. Shasta of northern California at 14,162 ft. with its five glaciers is dwarfed in size by Rainier, with its 36 square miles of ice, consisting of twenty-seven glaciers, of which six are major ones. Mt. Rainier has the deepest glacier, the Carbon Glacier, in the contiguous United States, measuring 700 feet at its deepest. Also, it has the Tahoma glacier, the largest glacier in the contiguous United States. The mountain as a whole contains an equivalent of one cubic mile of ice. From its many glaciers, major rivers are formed, providing the state of Washington with water, electric power, sports and recreation, and irrigation of farm lands as they work their way towards the Pacific Ocean some 100 plus miles away.

Not only is Mt. Rainier impressive size-wise, but also in the sport of climbing it offers almost everything that climber's desire in alpine climbing. Jim Whittaker, the first American to climb Mt. Everest in 1963 writes in his book *A Life On The Edge*, "Although Mount Rainier is only half as high as Mount Everest, altitude is all it lacks. Its glaciers and icefalls, its ferocious winds, and dangerous weather make it a near-perfect training ground for Himalayan expeditions, and it put us to the test." With its many available climbing routes, climbers can pick and choose from moderate to extreme in difficulty.

****

Hank Keeton and I have just driven the 145 miles from Salem, Oregon, to complete our second objective, that of climbing Mt. Rainier. We left Salem at around eight in the morning, after loading all our gear into my 1979 Volkswagen Camper Van. Our drive was an easy trip, taking us first through Portland, Oregon then into the state of Washington, all the while on Interstate Highway 5. Turning off the Interstate Highway onto smaller highways, we drove through small towns with names like Mossy Creek, Mineral, Elbe, and finally through Ashford, then to the entrance. The drive took around five hours to reach the west entrance of the park, and our plan was to find a camping spot in one of the park's regulated campgrounds for the night.

We pulled into Cougar Campground, selected a suitable site, and paid our overnight fee. Among our provisions, was an ample amount of food, including a cooler full of beer, and a portable Bar-B-Q with which to cook big juicy steaks. Our plan was to have a full dinner in the evening before our exhausting six thousand feet of elevation gain the following day, which would get us up to our bivouac site high on the mountain.

Since Mt. Rainier National Park has a check-in system for climbers, we decided to drive the remaining half dozen miles up the curvy road to Paradise Lodge, where we could check in with the ranger on duty. We also hoped to obtain an up-dated weather forecast.

Thirty minutes later we pulled into the parking area at Paradise Lodge, which is located at the end of the road, and as high as you can drive up the mountain. Paradise Lodge is located at five thousand four hundred feet, and at this time of year is teeming with tourists from all over the U.S. and many parts of the world, most hoping to get a close up view of the mountain. Many will be taking excursions, hiking up the plush meadows full of wild flowers, with cameras in hand, ready to take that prize-winning photograph. Some will be more adventurous, hiking up the snow, trying to get as high as safely possible on the flanks of the mountain.

The parking lot was swarming with climbers, most of them just returning from their summit attempts, sorting out,

and drying their climbing gear before heading back home. So many climbers! Hopefully, we won't be running into crowds like this on our selected route. Rationally, I know that the mountain belongs to all, but I always get this selfish feeling that I want it for myself.

The route we had chosen to climb is called the Kautz Glacier route. After reading the book "Challenge of Rainier" by Dee Molenaar, I fell in love with the description of this classic route. Even though it was not a technical route, the aspects of this climb intrigued me. We would be climbing on three major glaciers: the Nisqually, the Wilson, and the Kautz. Heading out at an elevation of five thousand four hundred feet, our bivouac site would be at 11,700 feet at a location called "Camp Hazard." Even though the name of this site sounds eerie, it is actually named after an early mountain guide named Joe Hazard. However, it is settled right beneath the Kautz ice cliffs, which tower some 300 to 500 feet above you, putting climbers in a precarious location for possible icefall. But, according to the guidebooks, most ice chunks falling off the cliffs fall to either side of the camp area. The next stage and possibly the crux of the climb takes you through the ice cliffs, then up a very steep section at the point where the glacier is at its narrowest. This section, under some conditions requires ice-screws or some form of protection. Above this steep climbing area, it is a matter of route finding, and following the glacier, hoping to avoid the many crevasses that are hidden, or open, by winding around, or even jumping them. Finally, you head to the main summit, named Columbia Crest, a huge snow filled crater, possibly two to three football fields wide in diameter. According to the book, "The Challenge of Rainier," the snow in the crater reaches a maximum depth of over 300 feet. The true summit requires trudging across this wide crater to the highest point on the northwestern point. Because of the dangers of descending later in the day under the thawing ice cliffs, and possibly having to down-climb steep ice, our plan was to take all our gear to the summit, and then descend by the easier standard route on the other side of the mountain.

We walked into the little ranger hut, located at the edge of the parking lot used for climber registration, and other information purposes. As we entered the building, we were greeted by a man dressed in a Smokey the Bear outfit, "Yes, may I help you?"

"We would like to register for a climb," I answered.

"Alright, read this information, and both fill out a card." Handing us the documents, he then asked, "Are there just two of you?"

"That's right," quickly responded Hank.

"Do you know how to do crevasse rescue, and do you have the proper gear with you?" The ranger continued to ask us questions with a hint of sarcasm in his voice.

"We are both trained in getting ourselves out of a crevasse, and have along prussiks and ascenders. Hopefully that's enough," I answered, slightly annoyed by the interrogation. He did not reply, probably thinking that we were just another pair of climbers asking to get into trouble.

The information sheet that we read contained a report of a climbing incident of the previous year, when a father and son were trapped on the summit for five days because of bad weather. During this time, ten feet of snow fell, and they barely survived the ordeal. Luckily for them, they had taken all their gear to the summit (tent, extra food, etc.), otherwise they would have died. This story eased my irritation with the ranger and I realized that he was just doing his duty in asking us the questions. With all the different climbers attempting this mountain, some experienced, others not, the park service has a difficult job trying to keep the wrong ones off the mountain. My biggest complaint though, was the manner in which some of them interrogated you. I'm sure that even Reinhold Messner, if wanting to climb this mountain would be given the third degree by a few of the more ego-oriented Rangers.

After filling out our cards and signing them, we handed them over to the ranger for his evaluation. Apparently, both of our climbing backgrounds were sufficient, and he approved our climb. We then asked him about the weather forecast, and he indicated that it wasn't too promising, with possible showers for the next day. After some questioning, he did indicate that the cloud ceiling was going to be around ten thousand feet, and that we might be able to get above the weather. After thanking him, we stepped out of the shack.

Since evening was approaching, it was getting cold and damp quickly. The fog was beginning to form nearly to the parking lot, the sun had already disappeared, and of course the mountain was hidden. We headed to the vehicle, and began our drive back down to our campground at Cougar for the night.

After an early dinner, and a few bottles of Rainier Ale, we climbed into the van, and quickly settled for the night. We knew that the next day would require all the energy that we could muster, and a good night's rest was needed. Climbing with full packs of approximately 50 to 60 pounds each, and an elevation gain of six thousand feet could sap even well-conditioned climbers of all their energy. As I lay there, listening to the sounds of other campers sitting around their blazing campfires, chatting and enjoying the cold crispness of the dark, fragrant forest, I thought about how nice it would be to join them, and stay up into the wee hours. Then, upon rising in the morning, cook the traditional breakfast of bacon, eggs, and pancakes, and spend the rest of the day just relaxing, reading, exploring, and watching the wild life in the park. Instead, I would be humping up steep, icy terrain, with my home and accessories for the next couple of days on my back, one minute soaking wet from the sweat, and the next, chilled through to the bone. But, I wouldn't trade anything for the coming adventure. With these final thoughts, I silently thanked the Lord for the opportunity, asked for his protection for both of us, and then fell soundly into sleep.

We arose at five a.m. in the morning. Opening the side door of the van, I quickly realized that it was a very misty morning, and that the clouds had descended to our level on the mountain. Quickly getting my boots, knickers, and a warm wool sweater on, I emerged from the vehicle. I immediately felt the sprinkles of cold rain, so I put on my wool cap and parka. The weather certainly didn't seem very promising at this point.

Hank joined me outside the vehicle, "What do you think about this stuff?"

"I don't know Hank. We'll just have to drive up to Paradise and see what it's like there. I just hope that it's not worse than this. This mountain is so unpredictable!"

"Should we fire up the stove?" Hank asked.

"Yeah! Let's take some time to have hot tea. We may end up just driving up to Paradise, and then turning around. Hopefully we can get some kind of weather forecast at the ranger hut, but I don't think they open until eight or nine in the morning."

We quickly fired up the gas stove in the van, and while heating the water had some cold cereal. After a couple of cups of hot tea each and then doing our "daily duty," we climbed into the van and headed up to Paradise Lodge.

It was just dawn as we drove into the immense parking lot, and up to the ranger hut. There was no sun on the horizon, but rather fog mixed with sprinkles of rain. We got out of the van, and walked up to the hut. There were no lights on inside, and a sign hung outside the door indicating that it would not be attended until eight a.m. The chalkboard hanging on the wall, showing the weather forecast, height of the cloud ceiling, and temperatures at

10,000 feet and 14,000 feet had not been up-dated from the previous day.

"You would think that someone could man this hut prior to eight in the morning," I commented. "Some people need to get started earlier than that," I added, knowing that it would take a very full day for us to reach camp Hazard.

"Typical government hours," Hank replied with a tone of disgust in his voice. "Well partner, what do you think?"

"The weathers not real bad. I suppose that we could head up and see what happens. I hate to have driven this far, and get turned back before we even get out of the parking lot."

Hank added, "The cloud ceiling was around ten thousand feet yesterday. If that's still the case, we might possibly get above it."

"You're right! Camp Hazard is at 11,700 feet, which is considerably higher than 10,000. I say let's give it a try. If we get forced down, we'll spend an evening in one of the local pubs."

"Sounds good to me boss! Let's try it!" Hank responded, with an optimistic tone in his voice.

I had to smile at his response. Even though it was only a few words, this was the answer that I was looking for. Most seasoned climbers are "eternal optimists," always looking for any little opportunity to advance further up a mountain. "I see a little bit of blue sky," or "I think the wind is beginning to die down," two common expressions that I have heard, or have even said myself a few times over the years. Maybe in climbing, it's because of man's constant battle with the elements of nature that he has to consistently search for the positive things in order to keep pushing ahead and not give up. Like any extreme physical sport, climbing is a constant mind game. "Keep going even if the body says No!" "Keep going even if your feet, face and hands are completely numb from the cold!" "Keep going even if the wind is gusting so hard that it throws you to the ground!" Or in extreme situations, "Keep going or you might die!"

Over the years, I have worked on keeping my mind in control of my body. From my early childhood, while working many long hours in the pear orchards of southern Oregon, bucking bales of hay in the hot summer months on a farm, or during the many hours working in the timber, I learned to keep going even when exhausted. I owe so much of my acquired stamina to my days in the Marine Corps. While on forced marches of over twenty miles, over hills, in sweltering heat, and full gear, I learned to put the pain and agony to one side, allowing the mind to dictate whether I quit or not. I always believed that I really didn't have much choice. This same attitude has been with me during my conditioning. For so many years, running has been the key to my conditioning. On many occasions, while running, and before the distance was covered, thoughts would come into my head telling me that I could stop short today, and just walk the rest of the way. Sometimes a side-ache would give me the same temptation, an excuse for stopping. This may be strange to some, but I never gave into these demands, always fearing that if I did it once, then it would be easier to give in the next time. And, that next time could be when your life was in jeopardy; during a hellish storm and lost on some mountain.

A few times in the past, I have been with climbers, who while caught in a bad storm wanted to give up, and sit down, "there and now," hoping for some kind of rescue. I acknowledge, there are times that you must dig in and wait it out. Many times, you must turn back, even though you don't want to. This is not what I'm referring to. In most tough situations, you have to reach inside yourself, and keep going. On one climb in particular, during a nasty storm and white-out, and on dangerous terrain, I had a couple of guys that wanted to give up, and hoped to be rescued in a place where rescue was out of the question. I had to get angry with them, telling them that they were acting like little old ladies, and ordering them to get on their feet and follow me, adding that *"sometimes, you just have to gut it out!"* They became so angry with me, and to spite me, they pulled it together, and we were able to work our way out of the situation. It was the anger that gave them the strength to do what they had to do. They had to prove to me that they could do it. I didn't like being put into the situation as the bad guy, but I had no choice. I'd rather climb with people that will do difficult things because they want to prove something to themselves, not to me or someone else.

Optimism; it is a huge factor in extreme sports. Why are some people optimistic, and others not? Why do some want to give up easily, and others don't? I don't know the full answer to these questions. It is probably very complex, and is tied into how our basic personalities are formed. Optimism may be directly attributable to our history of successes and failures. If our successes outnumber our failures, then possibly the result is that we are optimistic. But, both success and failure must be experienced to develop this trait. For example, if we have only successes in our lives, the first time that we truly fail we may not be able to rebound from it. If on the other hand, we have had mostly a life of failure, then our human spirit has been damaged to a point where success may mean nothing. Where and when do these experiences, which have a great effect on our personalities begin? I'm sure most of them occur at a young age when our parents are raising us. Understandably, parents need to praise the achievements and successes of their children. But, what about failure? It is equally important that parents handle these failures properly. I believe that many parents coddle their children too much, for example, picking them up each time they skin their knee.

Worse than that, they allow their children to give up when difficult problems arise, or during tough times. It is because of this protection that the child does not learn to deal with problems, or discomfort. Parents need to care and be sympathetic towards their child's hurts and fears, but must also allow the child to experience pain and discomfort, and to learn to overcome adverse situations on their own.

When it comes to climbing, and whom you pick for your climbing partners, it's important to pick out the right personalities. You try to choose those that will not give up in a tough situation, and who have that gift of optimism. Even though we had only climbed together on two mountains, I felt that Hank was the kind of climber that I could trust. Part of it was just a hunch, and part of it came from a few of the facts that I knew about him. For instance, while doing a solo rock climb, a ring hanging from a bolt from which he was resting on during his self-belay broke, and Hank fell around fifty feet. While in the air, he struggled to keep from landing on top of his wife who was picnicking below him, and at the same time to avoid some of the large rocks laying on the ground near-by. He landed on his feet, at a slight angle sending the shock up his legs to his back, thereby breaking his back. He survived the many weeks in the hospital, and as soon as possible, while even still in pain, began his comeback climbing. On our climbs together so far, I have noticed him stretching and dealing with that constant pain. Here is a person that deals with the pain constantly, but doesn't give up, knowing that if he wants to enjoy this type of adventure, he must put the pain out of his mind. This is the kind of person that I want to be with in adverse situations; a person that will not give up until the very end; and, a person with the *eternal optimism* that will find a way.

The parking lot was quiet this morning, with only a few climbers preparing to venture up the mountain. Even though it was a Monday morning, I was surprised that it was so quiet. Did someone know more about what weather was ahead on the mountain than us? After completing the sorting of our gear, we finished loading our packs. I was happy that the tent that I was carrying was so light, but a little concerned that if we ran into foul weather, we could be stuck like sardines in this little thing for a considerable time. Also, there would not be enough room for our packs and other climbing gear. Oh well, it was a little late to worry about that now.

After locking up the van, we hoisted the packs onto our shoulders, grabbed our ice axes and headed out. The first quarter of a mile or so of the hiking path is paved. It is such a strange feeling to be hiking up a black- topped path. It is also difficult, since as the angle increases, you are required to walk either on your toes, or like a duck, since there is no give in the surface. There was no one on the path this morning, attesting to the damp, chilly and foggy weather. We were getting slight sprinkles of rain, but the coolness felt good as our bodies began warming up carrying the heavy packs. There was a lot of snow just off the path, and I looked forward to getting up to the point where we would be off the path and entirely on the snow.

Soon we were at the area where the snow covered the trail, and we continued to go in the general direction of the mountain. Our first goal would be to find the vista where we would begin our descent down to the Nisqually Glacier. This was supposed to be a drop in elevation of around 400 feet to a point on the glacier where we would rope up, and cross the glacier to a steep chute on the other side. We would then have to climb this steep chute, traversing upwards towards the mountain in order to reach the Wapowety Cleaver. Once we reached the cleaver, we would follow it up until we got onto the Wilson Glacier. Moving along the upper side of the Wilson Glacier, and avoiding the many crevasses, we would approach the "turtle", a broad snow slope, consisting of a few tables, or layers, leading up to our high bivouac site just below the ice cliffs at Camp Hazard. Indeed, a very long way to go in one day.

Forty- five minutes later, the terrain was getting steeper, and I headed towards what looked like a steep edge to my left. There were still a few small trees in this area, but I could see that we would soon be leaving all the growth of the forest behind us. Now, to find the place where we head down to the glacier below. Just beyond the final trees looked like a vista that probably overlooked the Nisqually Glacier. Fifteen minutes later we reached the vista, and since we hadn't had a break, decided that this was a good time to take off our packs, and to wander over and see what was down the other side.

It felt good to have the heavy pack off my shoulders. I laid it down, then anxiously strolled over to the edge and peered down. There it was! The Nisqually! A magnificent glacier flowing down from near the summit of the mountain. You could see its jagged ice cliffs higher up and the enormous crevasses running at all angles through the glacier. Periodically, you could hear the crash of the ice as it came tumbling down off the ice cliffs, causing small avalanches of ice and rock flowing down the glacier until settling into a large crevasse. I peered down the side, directly beneath me. Too steep! This certainly wasn't the route down.

"Hank, I think we have to back track a little. We can't get down from here! Possibly a few hundred feet back near those trees we'll find a way down. Let's take a snack break here before we go any further."

"You bet! I could use some water about now. This Gore-Tex climbing suit seems to be a little warm right now," Hank said as he began un-zipping it for more circulation. "I hope that it was a good idea bringing it."

I had started off just wearing a wool cap, wool shirt, wool knickers and socks. It was perfect for the beginning, but as I sat there, I began to get cold, and I noticed that my clothing was pretty damp already. I had brought a 60/40 parka, so I pulled it out of my pack and put it on. These parkas were not water- proof, so hopefully we wouldn't be getting much more moisture as we climbed higher. Or if we did, I hoped that it would be in the form of the dryer snow.

Our break, during which we enjoyed the scenery, was short, and soon we had our packs on again, and began heading back down along the edge of the ridge, looking for the important

102

route down. Soon we came to a small trail through the trees, which looked to be the way. I followed it through the trees as it angled down. Yes! This had to be the way. As I looked ahead, I was surprised by how steep this section was. The snow was fairly soft, and the footing good, so I began traversing diagonally down, attempting to follow what looked to be a climber's trail with some boot tracks showing in the snow.

It had seemed so far down to the glacier, but within twenty minutes we were on the edge of the dirty and broken up ice. At this point, we pulled out the rope, uncoiling it. We put on our harnesses, and since we were going to be crossing on hard glacier ice, we attached the crampons to our boots.

"I believe that is the chute that we have to ascend, directly across the glacier from us. It also looks like we have some tracks to follow across this ice. Hopefully, we'll be able to cross this thing with no major problems. I could see where other climbers had left

boot marks on the ice nearly all the way across. It was a good feeling knowing that we were on track. After clipping the climbing rope to our harnesses, we attached the prussiks.

"I'm ready when you're ready," commented Hank.

"Well lets rock and roll," I responded enthusiastically. I felt charged, as we were finally off the well-beaten tourist paths, and heading across a great glacier.

It was fairly easy crossing the glacier at this point. The ice was very firm, and the crevasses small and highly visible. I was still being cautious, since there is always the potential for disaster on a glacier. I knew that Hank was alert to each of my steps, watching carefully, prepared to stop any kind of fall through the ice. It was level walking most the way across, so we were able to make good time. As we approached the other side of the glacier we had to skirt far around an enormous crevasse in order to gain the slope on the other side.

Soon, we were headed up the steep ice chute. It was nearly forty to forty-five degrees in steepness, and littered with rocks of all sizes that had probably fallen over the last few days, during the warm afternoons. I yelled back at Hank, "Keep an eye out for rock-fall! Another couple hundred feet and we'll be out this bowling alley."

"Got you, boss. Damn, this is hard work!" came back Hank's response.

It was hard work, lugging our heavy packs up this steep chute. Now and then there would be some steps made by previous climbers, but climbers sliding down the chute on their way back had torn most of them out. I had to kick fresh steps most of the way up. Soon, my throat was dry from the physical exertion, and I desired water to quench the thirst. Making it worse there was a small stream of melt off flowing down the chute beside me. Tantalizing! But, we would have to wait until we were in a safer spot before taking a break.

The chute curved toward the right, leading to a knoll with rocks. This looked like a good place for a break, and also a possible view of our route. It was further than I thought, and it took another fifty minutes before we finally reached the rocks. As Hank came up behind me, I pulled in the slack rope and laid it at my feet.

"Good place for a well-deserved break, Hank. Man, look at that view! Down there, you can even see our tracks all the way across the glacier."

"We've come a long ways! What a haul!" Hank added after glancing upward, "Too bad we can't see further up the mountain."

The clouds above were quite thick, and the visibility was probably only a thousand feet above us. Our route headed west of our current position, with another very steep snow slope to climb

104

up before reaching the Wapowety Cleaver. We had come a long way, but it was only the beginning. What an enormous mountain!

As we sat there, drinking the precious water and snacking, I thought to myself, *Just ten days ago we were on Mt. Jefferson, and here we are again, two small specks, on this great expanse of ice and rock, and completely alone.* The roar of small avalanches from the ice cliffs were much louder now that we were higher up the mountain and actually looking down at them.

It was around eleven a.m. when our break was finished, and we headed back up our route. The next section was a very long and straightforward trudge. In doing this stretch, there was no excitement, therefore no adrenaline flowing, making it boring and physically demanding. On top of that, it was beginning to sprinkle more, and the wetness began running down our faces into our eyes. An hour or so later we climbed the upper and steepest portion of the slope, and then found the terrain to be leveling off. In the distance I could see a large ridge of rock, and headed for it. *That must be the cleaver, I thought.*

As we approached closer to the rock, we began a traverse to the right, towards the mountain again, following the line of the ridge known as the Wapowety Cleaver. We were still angling upwards, but it wasn't as steep as below. The clouds still clung to the mountain, obscuring any view of the upper portions. If I hadn't had the route description firmly implanted in my mind, I would have sworn I was lost on this great mountain.

"Hank, we're at approximately 8,400 feet." I was glad that we were getting higher on the mountain, but with our destination today to be 11,700 feet, there remained over three thousand feet to climb. It meant that we had four or five more hours to go.

I'm not sure where the Wilson Glacier actually begins, but you know when you are on it by the sudden appearance of large crevasses. Staying high on the shoulder of the glacier, we worked our way along, around, and over the big deep cracks in the glacial ice. Ahead of us, and about a thousand feet higher was a large outcrop of rock. I estimated another hour or so to reach that point, so it was time for another break.

The sprinkles of rain were now turning to small particles of ice, or sleet, as the temperature had dropped several degrees from that below. We sat on our packs, taking in liquids, as well as candy and other snacks to refuel our bodies. It was amazing to look down on our route and see the distance that we had covered. How far was it to the ice cliffs and Camp Hazard? Since we couldn't see more than fifteen hundred feet, they were nowhere in view. With our short break over, we wearily got to our feet and headed up again.

The next thousand feet or so were agonizingly steep even though not technical. Every once in a while I would look up to see if the large outcrop of rocks was closer. Depressingly, they only seemed to get larger, not closer. Kick. Step up. Kick. Rest. Gulp down a few extra breaths, then kick. Step up.

As we approached the rocks, and knowing from the route description that many climbers spend the night here at approximately the 9,700 foot level, I thought to myself how nice it would be to make our camp here for the night. It was around three p.m., and we still had a long ways to go. Our goal was still the ice cliffs, so I tried not to rationalize an earlier camp.

As we headed up along the large outcrop of rocks, I thought I could see possible campsites among the smaller rocks. I thought, *If we have to bail off this mountain, this may be a place for an emergency camp.* Soon we were passing the last of the rocks, and could see ahead to our next objective. Another steep slope lay directly in front of us, and I guessed that this was the first table on the so- called "turtle."

Taking a short break, we then headed up the steep slope. I

was anxious to get to the top of this one, since there was a possibility that we would be able to see our objective from there. We were now around ten thousand feet, but still beneath clouds. Would we be able to get above these clouds?

As we were working our way to the top of the slope, the clouds seemed to thin, and I noticed I could see some blue sky. Halleluiah! Suddenly, we seemed to be getting above it.

"Hank, do you see what I see?"

"You bet I do! We're getting above this stuff."

Each few feet brought us a clearer view of what lay ahead. Now we could see the sunshine. Then, a few feet further, there suddenly appeared in the distance, the incredible Kautz ice cliffs. They had a brilliant light blue and white hue to them, and shone brightly in the sunlight like gems. Even from this distance, they looked gigantic and very imposing. There was no doubt in my mind we would have our bivouac just below these towering cliffs.

The next fifteen hundred feet in altitude probably covered a mile or so in distance. Our bodies were weary, and a cold stiff breeze made the going even more difficult. We were above the clouds and moisture, but I felt chilled from the dampness I had acquired down below. On we went, glancing up at the ice cliffs now and then, hoping to see them become closer.

At around seven, we finally arrived at our destination. Not knowing exactly the safest location for a bivouac site, we searched around, and finally found spots where other climbers had camped before. We were totally alone. No other climbers on this route today.

After picking out a good site, I quickly went about the business of setting up the midget tent, while Hank fired up the stove to heat the water for our warm meal. I felt half frozen, so I took off my wet parka, got into my pack and took out my wonderful heavy- duty goose-down parka. It's amazing how you can feel the warmth immediately forming in down clothing. Soon, my shivers were gone, and I sat and enjoyed my freeze-dried food in near total comfort. We sat there in awe at the beauty before us. Above us, the great ice cliffs. Below us, we could view the cleaver that we had climbed up along, and to our left, the Wilson and Nisqually glaciers. Almost directly across to the east, and a couple of miles away, we could make out the Muir snow field, and the approximate location of Camp Muir, the bivouac site for climbers on the standard route.

After our dinner meal, we took a stroll up to a point where we could get a better view of our route for the next morning. The description stated that you could either climb through the ice cliffs above, or drop down into the gully near us, climbing down a couple of hundred feet, then skirting around the ridge of rock and ice in order to gain the Kautz Glacier proper.

"I believe the best way is up through the ice cliffs, in order to avoid dropping down in elevation. What do you think Hank?"

"It's hard to tell from here, but I suppose we could check it out in the morning, seeing if we could spot the route through them," Hank replied.

"Yeah, it's getting a little dark right now, but we'll find out early in the morning. How about heading out of here around seven in the morning? With only less than three thousand feet elevation to go we should have plenty of time to reach the summit, and then descend down the other side to Camp Muir."

"That sounds okay to me. So far the weather is holding out up here." Hank added, "Hopefully, it will be nice tomorrow."

We quickly prepared our gear for the morning, and then crawled like sardines into the midget tent. We would have to endure another night in the tent. At least we were out of the wind. I thought, *Here we are, spending the night at nearly 12,000 feet, below giant ice cliffs, and on a route that neither of us had ever been on before.* What a great feeling! With those thoughts in my mind, I went quickly into a deep sleep.

We awoke around five a.m. The sun would soon be up, and it was already light. The wind was blowing gently, a very good sign in light of the fact that we were high on a mountain, and camped in a very exposed area.

I grunted my way out of the cramped little tent. Stretching, I looked around at the still incredible scenery. The sun would soon be hitting the top of the ice cliffs, and after that the warming would begin. A glance up towards the summit of the mountain indicated that it was free of clouds so far. A good sign! There were still clouds below us, but they hadn't crept up any higher. Another good sign! So far, so good!

"It's pretty nippy out here," I commented to Hank as he stood up, and also began to stretch his bad back. "The weather is looking pretty good so far. Of course we don't know what it's like on the summit, but from here it looks clear."

"Looks like there might be a slot through those ice cliffs," Hank commented, trying his best to describe the location he was looking at. "It ought to be very interesting trying to work our way through that area of ice. Maybe it will look better once we get up there."

"According to the guide, that's where most climbers traverse over to the glacier. Hopefully, there will be some kind of foot tracks up there to show us the way," I responded.

We soon had the stove fired up, heating up the water for the morning oatmeal and tea. While the MSR roared with its usual loudness, we went about tearing down the tent, and packing our packs for the climb. We were soon having our breakfast and enjoying the hot tea, as we gazed at the clouds below us.

"Just think Hank, people are still snug in their warm beds down there, while we are above the clouds, practically freezing our butts off." Are you sure this is the right hobby?"

"They can have their warm beds! I do miss being cuddled close to my wife though. But that can wait."

The sun was now beginning to touch the top of the 200-foot ice cliffs with its golden rays. Soon we would be feeling the warmth of the sun, and I was looking forward to thawing my hands and feet out. My gloves and boots were both still wet from the previous days rain.

Soon, we were hoisting our packs, and heading up to what looked like a good spot to either drop down into the chute or continue heading up towards the ice cliffs. I noticed that we were on solid rock, and there seemed to be tiers of it leading down to the chute. We stopped at a spot that seemed the easiest way down from where we were standing, in case we decided not to go further up towards the ice cliffs.

The ice cliffs were now fully visible with the sunshine glancing off them. It looked ominous, and I'm sure that we both had the same feeling that maybe we ought to be conservative, and climb down into the chute and do the end around, even though it would require losing altitude, surely taking more time.

"Let's get our crampons on. We'll need them either way," I commented.

As we put on our crampons, we glanced back and forth to the ice cliffs above, where we thought the crossing might be, then to the chute below us. It would probably take another twenty minutes to climb up high enough on the ice to begin our traverse.

If we couldn't get through there, then we would have lost a lot of valuable time, plus energy.

"I think I am for dropping down, and going around to the glacier. At least it will be a straight shot from there. Even if we can get through those ice cliffs, I'm not sure what we'll find on the other side trying to get onto the glacier."

We had made our decision. After getting our crampons on, I asked, "Okay! Are you ready? I'll start heading down this thing and see what the ice is like below us."

I was just about to take my first step downward when we heard a loud *"crack"* of a sound high above us. Quickly, we both looked up above us, and to our astonishment, a chunk of the ice cliff broke off and came tumbling and crashing down onto the snow, and then crashing into the chute. The roar was deafening, as the enormous piece broke into three or four smaller chunks of ice, each the size of a Volkswagen Beetle car, sweeping by directly in front of us through the chute below, followed by an avalanche of additional ice and rocks. The roar lasted only a few seconds, as it continued down towards part of the glacier.

I don't believe that my heart ever beat so hard! I could literally feel my heart in my throat. If, we had been only a few minutes earlier, they would have never found our bodies, since they would have been ground up like hamburger, then buried under tons of ice and rock. We were within twenty-five feet of never being seen again.

"Holy Moly!" I gasped, with my mouth wide open. I'm sure that I was wild-eyed as I stared down at the debris disappearing below.

"Sh—t Oh Dear!" came Hank's hoarse reply. What the hell caused that? I've never seen anything like that!"

"Hank, oh buddy, we just about bought it," I answered shakily.

As soon as my heart quit beating so hard, I was somehow able to regain my composure, even though my hands were still shaking. I believe that a lot of climbers would have turned around at this time and headed back. "Now what do we do?"

Hank responded, "I think that we ought to drop down from here and then cross over to the glacier. But, we certainly don't want to take our time about it!" He added, "I'm sure glad we didn't choose to go through those cliffs, because our trail went just below where that chunk broke off."

I agreed. We didn't hesitate but began carefully working our way down off the rocks to the ice below. As I left the rock, and touched the ice, I noticed that it was very hard ice, but mixed with rocks and dirt, giving a good texture for our crampons to dig into. We would have to be careful not to fall though.

"Hank, lets un-rope here. Its steep, but the footing seems to be good. Let's go one at a time. That way, if another chunk breaks off, it won't catch our rope and take us both at the same time. Watch and then follow me once I get out of the line of fire."

Hank began coiling the rope. I surveyed my potential route down along the rocks a couple of hundred feet, then to where I would cross the chute, and go around the corner of the outcrop of ice and rock. "Here goes nothing!" I exclaimed as I started down. The footing was good, so I sped up my pace, almost running down the ice with my crampons, but prepared to go into self-arrest if I fell. Once I reached the spot where I would make my 90-degree turn to the right and head directly across, I stopped. Looking back up at the ice cliffs above, I said a little prayer that God would protect me, and the ice would stay firm above. Taking a few quick gulps of air, I then trotted as fast as I safely could across the wide chute. It was approximately 150 feet across, and I made it safely to the bottom of the rocks, stopping at a point that I felt to be out of the fall line.

Out of breath, I yelled back at Hank, "Your turn buddy!" I then watched as Hank trotted down the steep ice, then across to where I was standing.

"Man, is it good to get across that in one piece," Hank exclaimed between gulping breaths of thin air.

We were both gasping for air, as one normally doesn't trot with a huge pack on at an altitude of nearly 12,000 feet. Hank uncoiled the rope, and we clipped in, ready to go around the corner, and head up the glacier.

Once we turned the corner, it was a straight shot up to the point just left of the ice cliffs, which is the narrowest and steepest part of the entire glacier. Even though we had lost 200 feet in our descent, it felt good to be able to see our objective ahead of us and to know that we would not have the ice cliffs directly above us.

As we climbed, the glacier became steeper, and as we approached the narrowest part, it reached 50 degrees in steepness. Some front pointing with our crampons was required over a stretch of forty to fifty feet, but soon after, the glacier began widening and leveling off to an easier angle. I noticed that gray dust covered the glacier the last few hundred feet. It dawned on me that it was from the eruption of Mt. St. Helens in May of this year, only two months prior. Even though most of dust from the eruption drifted east, much of it apparently was hurled north for many miles. What an eruption that must have been! Hank and I had climbed Mt. Hood in May, hoping to get pictures of the imminent eruption, but it didn't blow until the next day. We had missed it by less than one day. Finding a safe spot, we sat down and took our first break since heading out. The cold water felt good on our dry throats, caused by the exertion and the breathing of the dry cold air.

After fifteen minutes, we headed out again, winding our way through and around large crevasses. The crevasses were enormous, some probably thirty or forty feet wide, and over 200 feet deep. Peering down into these blue-green abysses made my adrenaline flow. They were so beautiful, yet could be so dangerous. The main danger didn't come from the crevasses you could see, but from the unseen ones. Climbers are not always aware that they are actually walking on snow bridges, with tremendous open depths below them. I probed my ice axe as I moved along, sensitive to any sudden softness in the texture of the glacier, a possible warning of a thin snow bridge beneath me.

I headed at an angle to the right towards a large cleaver of rocks, which was probably the top of the Wilson Headwall route. The Kautz Glacier becomes wider and actually expands across the end of this cleaver. Within another hour we had covered the distance, and were at the very end of the cleaver. We climbed up and off the glacier, scrambling through the rocks and dirt towards our next break area. We were now at about the 13,000 foot level, with around 1,400 feet in elevation remaining to the summit.

We sat mostly in silence as we viewed the route on which we had just come up. Looking across the crevasse covered glacier, we could look across from us and a thousand feet or more higher to Point Success. This was one of the three summits on Mt. Rainier. It was the second highest, after Columbia Crest, our destination. Liberty Cap on the north side of the mountain was the lower of the three, and we would only see it once we had reached the top of Columbia Crest. The weather remained clear, with a cold crisp breeze blowing. The clouds were still far below us, so the good weather seemed to be holding. At this point, I felt quite confident that we were going to get our summit today.

We hoisted our packs and headed out, feeling good that we would accomplish our goal today. We continued to traverse at a slightly right angle leading to an area less covered with crevasses, there the upper portion of the mountain seemed to take on a rounded appearance, indicating the final slopes to the summit crater. There were a few tracks, and in the distance I could make out a wand, or little red flag attached to a slender stick and stuck in the ice, seeming to confirm that we were heading in the right direction. These wands are useful in finding your way back if caught in a bad storm, or white out. Also, they are helpful in marking a crevasse, or snow bridge. Sometimes they served to show the way to go, and sometimes they were used as a warning to be cautious. We weren't carrying any of them on this trip, since we didn't plan on returning the same way as going up.

We seemed to be totally alone on the great mountain. There were no other climbers in sight. No fresh tracks. Just the two of us! We were two lonely specks in a world of white snow. As we worked our way up the glacier, I thought about how good it was to be by ourselves, away from other human contact. To see this beauty, and to know that just you and your friend are sharing this experience, and only as a result of your personal efforts, is truly a rewarding feeling. There is also an unsettling feeling that goes with it, knowing that if you get in trouble, there is no one to help you. That is the chance you take for this kind of thrilling experience. I knew that we were very self-sufficient, and I also knew that we were under God's mercy. It was good to be here, at this moment, and to be **breathing pure air**.

The crevasses were fewer, but very large, and sometimes very long. We spent considerable time finding our way around some of these crevasses. We had just wound our way around what seemed to be the bergschrund, our last major obstacle, and the remaining six to eight hundred feet seemed to be pretty straight upward, when the wind began to pick up considerably. Glancing up at the crater rim far above us, I noticed that thin clouds were beginning to flow across the summit. Was this a sign of a change in the weather? I hoped not!

Soon after, the wind was gusting hard enough to stop us in our tracks. We would take around ten steps, and then be stopped in our tracks by a strong gust of wind of at least forty miles per hour. Driving in our ice axes, we stooped low, trying to maintain a low profile, waiting for the gust to stop, and then we would proceed on again. It was hard work, and it took a lot of effort to move our bodies against the wind with our heavy packs on. ***Maybe we can get out of this stuff once we reach the crater,*** I thought to myself. The wind was biting cold, and I winced each time it blew against my bare face. I also noticed that my gloved hands, and the toes of my feet were beginning to get numb from the cold.

The next hour was miserable! The climber's old nemesis, "wind" was making our remaining few hundred feet an agonizing experience. On we went, forcing our way through the wind. The summit was now being quickly covered by a lenticular cloud, or cloud cap. A very bad sign! Lenticular clouds were almost always the sign of a major downturn in the weather.

Slowly, we went on. As we approached the summit crater, we found ourselves in the heavy cloud cap. The winds now were gusting close to sixty miles per hour, and we could barely fight our way through the rocks on the rim, then down to the crater floor and the snow inside the crater. The gusts didn't ease off as I had hoped on the crater floor. Hoping to find shelter on the other side of the crater, I yelled back at Hank at the top of my voice, "Let's keep going to the other side. Maybe we'll find shelter out of this wind next to the crater wall there."

I could barely hear his affirmative reply due to the roar of the wind. We continued slowly on, fighting to gain each few feet. The crater is two to three football fields in diameter, and it took quite some time to reach the other side. We found that the wind wasn't much better there, still threatening to flatten us out if we didn't carefully brace ourselves against it. I knew at this time, that we stood little chance of going down the standard route today. We needed to quickly find some way out of the wind, or chance hypothermia.

I was stopped by a gust of wind. I waited for it to subside. Frustrated, I yelled again at Hank, "Hank, lets unclip and drop this darn rope!" I was hoping that we could each maneuver a little easier without being attached to the rope, free to seek out some place to get out of the wind. I unclipped from the rope, and let it drop at my feet, thinking that there was no danger now that we were no longer on the glacier. We had reached an area probably a hundred feet from the rocks on the side of the crater.

I began walking parallel to the rocks, looking for a shelter in the rocks, or possibly a spot to pitch our little tent out of the direct wind. I was nearly exhausted from fighting the wind for so long, and getting very cold. I struggled forward, now dragging my ice axe behind me, grasping the adze, the wider portion of the ice axe, opposite from the pick. Out of the corner of my eye, I caught a glimpse of Hank closer to the rocks than me, but only approximately twenty feet away.

Suddenly, I broke through the crust of the icy snow. In a split second, as my body began falling through the large hole, my arm instinctively shot forward, sliding the shaft of the axe quickly through my open hand until it was stopped by the safety ring. The sharp point of the pick seemed to grab the ice on the surface a few feet ahead of the hole. In that same split second I saw below me a black bottomless void. My body was half way through the hole, when the pick grasped the ice, and simultaneously my legs came flying up behind me, and out of the hole. I was next to the manhole-sized hole that had a crust of six to eight inches thick. I crawled on my stomach in a swimming motion trying to get away as quickly as I could. As soon as I felt that I was a safe distance from the hole, I just lay there for a while, almost paralyzed by the fear of what had just happened. This was the second time today that I had looked death in the eye. Shakily, I managed to get to my feet.

Hank had seen the whole thing. "Are you okay?" he yelled.

I was gasping for breath and just stood there recuperating. After gathering some strength, I slowly made my way cautiously over to where Hank was standing. "Wow! I can hardly believe it

Hank, but I nearly fell all the way through that hole into the depths below!"

"I saw it! I really thought you were a goner, and there wasn't a damn thing I could do about it! Hank exclaimed apologetically. "How in the hell did you get out of it? I've never quite seen anything like it."

"I don't know Hank! It happened so fast! I threw the ice axe forward and the pick grasped the ice, but my legs just came flying out of it! There was no effort involved. It's a miracle! And you're right; I believe that I would have been gone for sure! That seems to be a bottomless hole, possibly the inside of the crater below the ice, probably dropping downs hundreds of feet."

As we both stared at the hole a few yards away, Hank added," Well boss, I'm damn glad that you survived. Besides, I wouldn't want to try getting down this mountain by myself nor spending the night up here alone. After pausing a moment, "Well, I guess we had better find a place quick in which to get out of this wind."

I was still shaky and weak at the knees, but agreed with his suggestion. Hank decided to go over to an area where the crater ice was clinging up the wall of the crater, to look for some kind of ice cave, while I decided to explore for a platform in which to set the tent up.

Making sure that I was a safe distance from the hole and what lay beneath it, I found a fairly level spot, and began leveling it out more with my ice axe. I glanced over and could see Hank chopping away with his axe, trying to break through into some kind of space behind the thick ice. Soon, he had a hole, crawled in and disappeared from sight. In a few minutes he was sticking his head out, and yelled that he was going to take the stove inside, fire it up, and try to melt snow for hot water. I yelled back my approval, and continued to work on my project, the tent site, and getting the tent set up.

My mind kept going back to the recent occurrence, and I would glance over to where I could still see the hole. Shivers ran down my spine when I thought of how close I came to disappearing, possibly forever into the darkness. I got back to the business at hand, and continued working in the heavy gusts of wind, while Hank remained hidden in his ice cave. Every once in a while, when the wind would die down, I thought I could hear Hank cussing at something. After creating a level platform, and before I attempted to put the tent up, I decided to venture over to his cave and see what was going on. When I reached the cave, and peeked my head inside, I could barely see him in the dark. "How's it going?" I asked.

"This damn stove keeps going out on me and I can't seem to figure out why," he answered back. "But don't worry, I'll keep working on it."

He didn't look too comfortable in there, as it looked like he was sitting on a steep incline of rock and dirt, just below the slanting wall of ice. He had the stove propped up in a precarious position with an assortment of rocks. I was glad that he was in there, and not me. I told him I was going back to the tent, wished him good luck, and headed back into the cold wind. At least he was out of the elements.

By the time I had finished my struggle of getting the tent set up, Hank had managed to figure out the problem with the stove, and was in the process of boiling the melted snow water. I struggled back to the ice cave, and crawled in.

"Welcome partner! The water will be hot in a minute. Come over for some hot tea, but be carefully that you don't fall down into whatever lies beneath us."

Great, I thought! Now we're sitting on the side of an abyss. Oh well, it was wonderful getting out of the wind, and I worked my way over carefully to where Hank and the stove were operating. I looked forward to something warm to drink.

As I drank my cup of Lipton tea, I began to feel life, and to a great extent, optimism flow back into me. We had gotten out of the storm. Hank, with his *never give up* attitude had managed to figure out the problem with the stove, which was caused by over pumping it, and having too much pressure in the fuel tank. Once he let the pressure out, and re-pumped it a few times it worked fine. Our altitude, causing the change in the pressure was the problem. I probably would have never figured it out by myself. Now, we were putting life sustenance back into our bodies. After finishing the tea, we chose to share a freeze-dried meal and a couple of whole-wheat rolls. A perfect meal, considering where we were! With our headlamps on, we stared down at the rocks and the darkness below us, under the illumination of the sloping roof of ice. Strange shadows danced around as the light from our headlamps glanced off the icy walls. We dared not move too much, fearful that we would lose our stove or some of our gear down below us. Even worse, we didn't relish the thought of sliding off into space. What a place to share a meal!

We discussed the alternatives, of which there really weren't any, except to spend the night on the summit and wait out the storm. Hopefully by morning the storm would have passed by, and we would be able to descend down the standard route. In the back of my mind, I was reminded of the father and son who spent five days up here, trapped in a storm. Knowing that I didn't relish the idea of doing the same, I quickly put it out of my mind.

It was nearly dark when we emerged from our little ice shelter. It was very cold, and very windy. I reached into my pack, and again took out my down parka, replacing the cold damp parka that I had been wearing. I had been keeping my down parka protected from the dampness for just this occasion. I decided that I would also wear it to sleep in. The combination of my down bag and the down parka would keep me adequately warm through the night.

Again, we squeezed into the small tent and slid into our sleeping bags. As we lay there, we could hear the wind howling outside. It would seem to go all the way around the crater, return, and then nearly knock our tent down. It was a constant cycle. This went on most of the night. It was freezing cold outside by now, and when the moisture from our breaths formed on the inside of the tent, it would turn to ice. Each time the blast of air would hit our tent, it would shake the ice off, causing it to fall in our faces, startling us, and waking us up. We were safe and warm, but it was indeed a fitful night of sleep for both of us. As I lay there, I prayed that the storm would subside, and that we would be able to go down the mountain the next day.

We awoke early the next morning. The wind had died down! As we opened the flap of the tent and peered out, we immediately saw that it was sunny! Crawling out of our tents, we felt the crisp, coldness of the summit air. Stiffly we moved about, trying to stretch our bodies, and again fired up the stove, and prepared our warm meal. Soon we would begin our descending the mountain. The weather was clear and beautiful. Looking around, I knew that we were the only ones to have spent the night on the summit of Rainier. We had survived an ordeal together, as buddies.

While we ate, mostly in silence, I again looked around us, trying to take in all the beauty of this beautiful morning. I tried also to recall each moment of the previous day. Not too far away I could see the hole, which I nearly disappeared into. While gazing at this strange and eerie thing, a wonderful warm feeling came over me, awakening me to the fact that I had survived something, when in fact I shouldn't have. There is no way that I could have pulled myself out of that hole, in that manner. I knew in my heart, that I had survived because of a miracle! Quietly, and with a humble heart, I thanked the Lord for sparing my life. Not once, but twice, in one day. A verse from the bible then came into my mind, one that I had read after surviving another fall years earlier. Psalms 91:11&12 reads, *For he will command his angels concerning you, to guard you in all your ways, they will lift you up in their hands, so that you will not strike your foot against a stone.* Truly, this had to be the answer!

After eating, we packed up and again hoisted our packs. Before heading down, we took out a camera, photographing our ice shelter, and the hole that I nearly fell through. Saying good-bye to the mountain, we headed back across the crater to search for the way down by the standard route. As we climbed over the rim, I headed in the general direction that I guessed was the way down since I had climbed the standard route twice before. Soon we came across a wand waving in the breeze. This must be the way! Carefully we worked our way down around the large crevasses, sometimes jumping the smaller ones. We continued heading down towards Disappointment Cleaver, which I could see in the distance, the route off the mountain that I was familiar with.

We continued at good speed down the moderate slopes. We were almost trotting down the slopes when we came upon a group of climbers climbing up the route. As we sped by them, they just seemed to stare, probably thinking that we were a couple of loonies who had lost our way. Within an hour or so were just above the cleaver, at approximately 13,000 feet. Just below us was a steep section that had a chute, which was made by previous climbers glissading down the slope. It looked safe, and would certainly provide a much quicker means of getting down the next two or three hundred feet.

"Hank lets glissade this section. It will save wear and tear on the body." I moved downwards a distance, then stepped into the chute, sat down, holding my ice axe as a rudder, and prepared to slide down the slope. Hank also stepped into the chute, forty feet above me, and prepared to glissade

"Whoopee!" I yelled as I began my slide. I could feel the slight tug on Hank, and soon both of us were sliding quickly down the man-made slide. Near the bottom there was a slight buildup of snow in my path, but I plowed right through it, not realizing that a crevasse was right below it. My speed carried me over it down to the other side. I quickly jumped to my feet, and yelled back at Hank to warn him about the crevasse, but either he couldn't hear me, or his speed was too fast to stop. He also went flying over the crevasse. The difference was that while in mid-air, the thin snow bridge collapsed under his weight. His momentum carried him safely over the snow bridge, as hundreds of pounds of snow crashed down inside the crevasse. We both just stood there looking at the now open crevasse, and then began laughing uproariously. We had survived so much on this trip that things were beginning to seem hilarious to us. No doubt about it, it was time to get off this mountain!

The rest of the descent was without incident, and several hours later we were back at the parking lot at Paradise Lodge. We had reserved a room at the lodge for that night, and after a wonderful warm bath, we spent the evening having a steak dinner at the lodge dining room, sharing a fine bottle of wine and planning our next climbing adventure.

The next morning the weather was beautiful and warm. As I sat outside, in the hewn out heavy wooden chair on the deck surrounding the lodge, soaking up the sun, and drinking a cup of coffee, I viewed the magnificent mountain, and its gorgeous surroundings of snow, trees and wild flowers. As tourists walked close by, I could hear one of them say, "I wonder if that's the summit way up there?" Another one, "How long does it take to hike it?" Another one, "Why do you suppose those climbers carry such large packs?" And, "Do you think there might be a road taking you to the top?" As I listened to these conversations, a smile came to my face and I thought, *If they only knew!*

CHAPTER V

ROYAL FLUSH
ROYAL ARCHES-ROTTEN LOG ROUTE

It was during June, 1981 that my friend and climbing partner Hank Keeton, whom I had led up two difficult and exciting climbs in the Northwest, asked me to meet him in Yosemite Park to do something **really** spectacular. He was living in Berkeley, California at the time, and as he had been weaned as a climber in Yosemite and other nearby Sierra climbing areas, he wanted to show me another aspect of climbing; **good rock.** Most of the rock in Oregon is very rotten, and unless you climb on it often, it has the tendency to freak you out. Since I was leading a Mt. Shasta climb in early June, he invited me to join him afterwards at Yosemite National Park for a couple of days of rock climbing. I agreed, knowing that this might be my only chance to ever climb on beautiful granite with a "camp four" veteran. Camp four is referring to the camping area where the "old salts" or Yosemite climbing veterans have hung out for many years. All experienced valley climbers can tell you where camp four is located.

The group I was leading up Mt. Shasta, the 14,162 ft. giant located in Northern California, was from the Chemeketans, a Salem climbing club. My fourteen year old son Mark was going to accompany me on this climb, not planning to go to the summit, but only going to base camp for experience. The base camp is located at 10,499 feet at a place called Lake Ann.

The weather was good, and we accomplished the climb in the normal two days. We did have quite a work-out on our summit day, as our group was not only enthusiastic, but also competitive, each being experienced mountaineers and in very good condition. The weather and snow conditions were good, and it seemed that we were racing for the summit. I enjoyed the intense work out, and the competition, not realizing that I should be saving strength for the adventure that would be following in a couple of days.

After returning from the summit, everyone was exhilarated, but totally drained of energy. Upon reaching base camp, we still had ahead of us the packing of our gear, and the several miles hike out. After being up in the cold fresh air, our camp seemed to be stifling hot, and it sapped our remaining energy to break down the camp. We finally hoisted our packs, and began our trek down the soft snow to the parking lot and the awaiting cars. An hour and a half later we arrived at the vehicles. We were spent! Our bodies were aching, and the extreme heat made the end of our climb miserable. After congratulations, and shaking of hands and hugs, we threw our gear into the vehicles and parted.

My son and I searched around in Shasta City and found an inexpensive motel to stay in, since we would be heading south to Yosemite the following morning. The motel had a nice swimming pool, and even though my thoughts had been of taking a cool swim while we were baking at base camp, I found myself too exhausted to even consider a swim. After showering, I dropped onto the bed, and it felt like a soft cloud, easing the aches and pains in my body. After a short nap, my son and I headed out to see if we could find some enticing food. We found the pizza parlor where some of our group had mentioned going earlier. Upon entering the establishment we realized that everyone had probably headed back north, to their homes. We didn't care, as long as there was pizza available. After we had stuffed ourselves with the wonderful tasting carbohydrates, we headed back to the motel, hoping for a good night's sleep, knowing that we would have a six hundred mile drive the next day.

****

The next morning I awoke stiff and tired. It seemed that the weather was extremely hot that morning, and later we found out that all of Northern California was having a heat wave. Temperatures around Sacramento were near 110 degrees. I was hoping that it would be cooler at our destination in Yosemite Park, which is located at a much higher elevation.

The V.W. pickup that was nearly new didn't seem to want to run that morning, but we managed to get it started and drove it to the restaurant for our breakfast. After breakfast, it would not start. It had a diesel engine, something that I knew even less about than the standard gas engine. What to do? In the back of my mind was the six p.m. meeting with Hank at the gate to Yosemite Park. I was worried. We searched around and found a parts store that was open. I needed some help quick! Fortunately, the store business was slow on this Sunday morning, and an employee, who seemed to know something about diesel engines, went to my VW, opened my hood, and tinkered around to see what was wrong.

It didn't take him long to come to the conclusion that I had water in the diesel, probably caused by buying my diesel fuel at a cut-rate station before the trip. After he cleaned out the fuel lines, we were successful in getting it started. It was still running rough, and he suggested that we go to a station on the outskirts of town and fill the vehicle up with good diesel. I thanked him, and away we went.

The station was located north of town, opposite the direction that we were going. It would take extra time, but we had little choice. The engine coughed and sputtered as we made our way out of town to the truck stop. I was wondering if we would make it that far, but we finally limped into the service station.

While filling the vehicle with clean fuel, I described the problem to the attendant at the station. He suggested adding an alcohol derivative to the diesel to get rid of the water. I decided he knew what he was doing, and had him add it to the fuel. After some time letting it mix with the fuel, we tried again. It worked! The derivative apparently got rid of the water. Soon we were off, and heading speedily along the highway toward Sacramento.

As I was driving, I tried calculating in my mind how long it would take us to get to Yosemite. I quickly reached the conclusion that we would not make it by six o'clock p.m. A bigger problem was that there was no way to contact Hank and tell him we would be late, and I found myself frustrated and worried that we wouldn't connect. This was before the days of the cell phones, and there was no way of getting a hold of him. I told my son Mark that we were going to drive about as fast as that diesel engine would allow us, and I appointed him as point. (**Point** in military terms refers to the men assigned to be up front during a patrol watching for the enemy). I gave him a pair of binoculars and told him to watch ahead for the police. Indeed, not a good lesson for a fourteen year old!

We arrived at the park entrance to Yosemite at nine-thirty p.m., three and one half hours late. Now, how to find Hank?

No one was at the entrance. I looked around and noticed a bulletin board with what looked like many scraps of paper attached to the board with messages on them. I got out of the vehicle and walked to the bulletin board. I scanned the many messages, and luckily spotted a note from Hank. The message from Hank said that he would meet us in Yosemite Village, and he gave a cabin number. Thank Goodness!

By the time we got to the village, it was after ten p.m. Finding the cabin was not easy, since it was dark, and we were in completely unfamiliar territory. I believe that it was pure luck that we stumbled upon it. Hank was elated that we made it. He welcomed us with a hug, and then opened a couple of beers. After explaining the day's events, we spent the next hour or so discussing the next day's agenda. Most of the planning was a mere blur, but I forced my eyes to stay open, and tried to respond with some intelligence. Finally, we called it an evening, and headed for bed.

Mark and I were exhausted, especially me, and I was grateful that we were not going to do any serious climbing the next day. Hank suggested that the next day after breakfast we go out and do a little warm up on "**Manure pile buttress**," or Ranger Rock as it is more commonly called. It was a huge rock with many routes of several rope pitches, or rope lengths. It would be good training for me to do something a little more difficult than I was used to in the northwest, and of course on granite. Afterward, we would take a dip in the beautiful Merced River. All the time Hank was discussing our plans, my body was saying **why don't you just hang out at the lodge and take life easy?** I thought about it, but knew that I wouldn't, since once you have the disease called "climbing," it constantly urges you into your next objective. We were in bed at twelve thirty, and soon snoring.

The next morning we arose at seven o'clock, and headed over to the lodge restaurant. I enjoyed a healthy breakfast of pancakes and eggs, and many cups of hot coffee. It would take all the caffeine I could get to jump-start my body. I was tired and my body was so stiff from climbing Mt. Shasta that it was difficult for me to even walk. Being so tired, I could barely climb class 5.4 or 5.5. and today would be much more difficult.

We did manage to do some short climbs, but I was relieved when Hank said, "It's getting too damn hot, let's go take a dip in the river!" Pleasing words to an exhausted partner.

The cold pure water of the Merced River seemed to revitalize me. It numbed my body enough that I could not feel the soreness. Energy began flowing back into me. We spent a long time in that beautiful green colored water. I didn't want to leave. The beauty in Yosemite can hardly be matched anywhere in the world. As described by Michael Borghoff:

Look well about you, wanderer! There is but one
Yosemite on the face of the earth,
And through the myriad moods, the shifting
Cyclic patterns, will always sound
The chord of this, your need: simple
Joy and certitude, the face of life itself.

It is a world apart from anything. Looking around me at the beautiful granite rock faces, and the plunging waterfalls brought even more life into my tired body. I stood there, up to my waist in the river, mesmerized by the beauty, and my spirit was lifted!

Alas, Hank again brought me back to reality. "Hey partner, which one would you like to climb? You have your choice. Make it a good one!"

I replied, "I don't know. What do you suggest?"

We got into the vehicle and drove to an area where we had a view of most of the major rock formations, all the way from El Capitan to Half Dome. He pointed out the various climbs in the valley, giving me a brief description of each, including various routes. Hank suggested that we do a grade III climb, difficult enough so I could appreciate the enormity of Yosemite's walls. Grade III is rated as an all-day climb, not extremely difficult for seasoned rock climbers, but difficult enough to thrill a rock climbing novice like me. I asked him to point out some grade III climbs to me. When he pointed to a gigantic wall with dark swooping arches, and

129

told me about its features and some of its history I quickly responded, "That's the one!"

It was named Royal Arches, the "rotten log" route. Not only was it a beautiful and impressive looking rock face of 1,300 ft., but it was considered a **"classic climb,"** being written up in the book "Fifty Classic Climbs Of North America" by Steve Roper and Allen Steck. Many climbers such as myself had goals of doing some of the climbs illustrated in this popular book. This specific climb was famous for its unique features, mainly the "rotten log." The climb has two sections where you either do a pendulum (swinging or running back and forth hanging on a rope which has been attached to an anchor, until you reach a ledge or other obtainable goal) or you free climb the same almost impassable sheer blank section of rock but with very few hand and footholds. Once past the second pendulum you come to an old rotten log perched across a chasm, approximately 800 ft. above the valley floor, with nothing but air below you. The log is leaning at a thirty to forty degree angle from one side of the chasm to the other. This log has very few limbs, but mainly knobs where limbs used to be. You have to cross this log!

"Royal Arches!" This would be a nice climbing experience to have had. It's amazing how bold one can be looking up at something a mile or so away. The decision was made. We would head out about seven in the morning. If we moved fast, we could have the climb completed in eight hours.

****

It was still unusually warm that morning. I was hoping that there would be a breeze up higher helping to make it cooler on the face of the climb. We arose early that morning, had a quick breakfast at the lodge, and after clearing out our cabin and loading everything into my pickup, we bade

130

Mark good-bye.

"Mark, here are the keys to the pickup. If you go someplace, be sure to lock up the vehicle, and **don't leave the keys inside!**" I added "here's a few dollars for lunch, drinks, or whatever else you need. We should be back fairly early, but if we're late, just wait at the pickup for us."

Mark assured us that he would be just fine, and told us to have a safe climb. I'm sure that he was anxious for us to leave since the valley was full of nice looking young women.

We took Hank's V.W. Bug and drove to the parking lot at the Ahwahnee Hotel, which is close to the trail taking you to the beginning of the climb. The signs all around the parking lot indicated "no parking" except for customers of the hotel. Oh well! It was too late to worry about that now. The temperature was rising and we needed to get started. Hoisting our packs, then placing the runners laden with rock climbing gear such as chocks, nuts, friends, stoppers, and extra slings around our necks, and lastly the climbing rope, we began our short hike to the base of the climb. The weight of all the gear burdened me, and I was grateful that we would not be carrying the 150 ft. climbing rope very far since it was so heavy. You could see that the hiking trail was well used. Within five minutes we were at the base of a long slanted chimney, the beginning of the climb. It looked like we had this chimney all to ourselves, even though we could hear some climbers far above us yelling out commands.

Nervously, I eyed the four-foot wide chimney. It was steep and long, probably near a hundred feet high. I had never climbed a true chimney such as this, only practicing on short wide ones. We laid out the rope, put on our climbing harnesses and again slipped the slings loaded with gear over our heads. My mouth was already dry from the anxiety, and my stomach was beginning to churn. I was happy that Hank was going to lead all of the pitches that day, not only since he was familiar with the route, but wanted to insure that we moved rapidly throughout the climb in order to finish before dark. I found a good belay spot, paying out the rope to Hank.

"See you later buddy," Hank said as he began moving up the four-foot chimney.

I watched intently at his style and movements, hoping that I could do the same thing. Soon he was out of sight, almost straight above me, but I could feel the slight tug on the rope as he moved up.

I heard him yell down at me, "I'm above the chimney, but will go up a little further to a good belay spot." The rope continued to slide through my hands as he went higher. There were only fifteen to twenty feet left of the rope on the ground when he stopped. I waited and listened.

A little while later he yelled down to me, "**On belay!**"

I yelled back, "**Belay on! Take up rope!**" Soon the slack in the rope was pulled up and I was ready to climb. "**Climbing!**" I called out.

I soon received the affirmative reply from above, "**Climb!**"

It was now my turn going up this long chimney. I squeezed into it. I put one hand against the rock in front of me, and the other hand against the rock in back of me. I firmly pushed against the rock, and then placed my right leg up against the rock higher in front of me, bending my knees. I placed my left leg behind me, with my feet flat against the rock. I then straightened the leg in front of me, pushing upward with my rear foot. This action caused me to move upwards. If either of my feet began slipping, I could just add pressure against the rock and it would stop. It was hard for me to believe I was actually moving upwards.

Sometimes, I would reverse the order of my legs and feet, trying to prevent the muscles from becoming exhausted. In the wider part of the chimney I had to put both feet in front of me, with both hands pushing against the rock behind me. Hank kept the rope snug, which gave me a feeling of security. It was difficult work, especially with the pack scraping against the rock behind me. I just hoped that the movement was not tearing my pack apart. The next fifteen minutes or more I grunted and scraped my way up this chimney, only looking down occasionally at the void below me.

I was wet with sweat, and my mouth was exceedingly dry when I finally reached the top of the chimney. I felt good though, knowing that I could do something completely new.

I heard Hank above me yell, "Good job, Metternich! How did you like it?"

"It was great! What's next?"

"The next few pitches are fairly easy, almost like scrambling," Hank said in a tone of reassurance. "We should be able to move quite quickly."

The next part of the climbing was fun, not being very steep, and with with exceptional cracks and hand holds. We moved quickly over the easy granite. One section had what was called the bear hug, where the rock bulged out, and you actually hugged it on both sides with your hands approximately two feet apart as you moved upward. Then we came to a large ledge where Hank belayed me up to him. We drank some of our precious life sustaining water, then, looked up at the next section.

"I don't remember this crack, but we should be able to do it okay," Hank said.

Above us was a very steep pitch with a nice finger crack in it. There was a piton placed in the rock ten or twelve feet above us, about midway. The piton should have given us a clue to the difficulty ahead, and the possibility we were off route.

When we were ready, I again let out some slack, and Hank began his ascent up this crack. He was almost to the piton when he let out a cuss word, and told me he was coming down. I lowered him back to where I was belaying. "Damn, that is tough! I just don't remember anything that difficult this far down." After catching his breath, he said, "Oh well, I'll try it again. **"Climbing!"**

Again, he made it to about the same spot, but then yelled down for me to lower him. "Wow! I must be out of shape. Metternich, I know that it isn't ethical, but I'm going to grab that piton this time. We could waste our whole day here if I don't."

I agreed, "I won't tell if you don't."

This time Hank took a few quick steps, then half ran up the rock, and when reaching the piton, grabbed onto it for support. Soon he was above it and began moving again smoothly up the rocks. After another hundred feet or so he found a belay spot, and was soon yelling down for me to climb.

I was nervous! Could I get up this pitch? I had to, since I didn't have any choice! I took a few quick steps, quickly moving up the lower portion and soon grabbed the piton for support. I reached above the piton finding a good crack and pulled myself up and away from that steep section. "**Holy Moly**," that was tough. In my mind I was thinking, *Will I be able to do the rest of this climb?* I quickly moved up to where Hank was belayed. We later found out that we were actually off route, and had probably done a 5.9 section of climbing.

Upward we climbed, now getting to a point where the bare section of the wall that would need a pendulum was getting closer into view. The last section up to below the pendulum was again smooth. It started off with good cracks to put your fingers into, but then the cracks suddenly disappeared and the remaining forty or fifty feet was a bulged out, smooth friction pitch. Hank didn't seem to have any problem getting up this long pitch, and then settled into a notch with some small bushes around him.

Again, I heard that familiar phrase, "**On Belay!**"

At first I moved rapidly up the cracks. I was getting to be an old hand at this now. When the cracks suddenly diminished, then literally disappeared, I found myself on scary, smooth, and bulged out granite. Hank was tugging on the rope, so I just kept moving, trying to get my climbing shoes to mesh onto the rock. I moved up another fifteen feet, and then my feet began slipping away. I tried stopping and adjusting my soles flatter to the rock, but I continued to slide a few inches. I decided to keep going for it, speeding up the pace in order not to slide off. Miraculously, I kept moving, and soon I had ascended above the smooth granite and onto rock with more cracks. A few minutes later I was sitting down next to Hank who had found a comfortable belay spot where we could both take a break.

"Hank, I damn near slid off down there! How did you do it so easy?"

"Partner, I was sliding too, but I had no choice, and had to keep moving, just like you!" Hank answered matter of fact. "Next, you are going to have a real thrill! Just up above us I will clip into that bolt, and then we will do our first pendulum.

"Where do we pendulum to? I don't see any ledge up there!" I asked with concern.

Hank answered, "There is a small one that you will eventually swing up to. Once you grab it, you can pull yourself up and onto it."

"Sounds crazy! Man, am I thirsty! It must be over a hundred degrees up here! How do the other climbers manage this heat?"

"They don't" answered Hank. Most of the hotshot climbers in the valley are not climbing today. It's too damn hot!" He added, "I'm quite surprised there are climbers on this route today. They were smart and had a much earlier start. We should have probably done the same."

I was tired, hot and sweaty, and extremely thirsty. I knew that I needed to reserve my next quart of water, so I drank sparingly. I also tried to get some food into me, as I knew I would need the energy. It was difficult eating the cheese, and gorp with such a dry mouth, but I forced myself. My legs were shaking, probably from the tiredness, but I felt competent that as soon as we began climbing again, the adrenaline would begin pumping through my veins, giving me that extra energy that I so badly needed. I suddenly became aware that I was getting blood all over my clothes from my hands where the skin had been torn off by the sharp rocks in the cracks we had climbed. It didn't hurt, but it sure looked bad. If that's the only thing that happens to me today, I will consider myself fortunate. The view from our position was indescribable! We could see most of the valley below us. Winding its way through the trees was the Merced River. The Great rocks such as El Capitan, Half Dome, Sentinel, Cathedral Rock and others could also be seen from here.

After our break of fifteen minutes or so, Hank told me to belay him as he was going to climb up to the bare section and clip into the bolt. Instead of hammering in pitons, holes are drilled by climbers and then long bolts are screwed in. These bolts are placed in areas of very difficult climbing, to be used only for protection against falls, and to aid climbing pitches such as this one. On the end of the bolt is a part called a hanger, from which you clip your carabiner into. Soon he was on belay and climbing up. He clipped the rope into a new runner he had hung from the bolt, then pulled the rope down, giving himself enough slack in the rope to begin his back and forth movement underneath the bolt. Soon he was running back and forth until he had enough momentum to reach up and grab the ledge with one hand. He then placed his other hand on the ledge, and pulled himself up, first on a knee, then standing up. He moved forward on the ledge until he found a good crack to place protection, and then secured himself into the protection so that he could belay me up. Now it was my turn!

The adrenaline was now pumping throughout my body, giving me the energy I needed to continue. I climbed up to the spot where Hank began his pendulum. I looked at the smooth blank wall that had to be crossed. It was nearly vertical, and from where I stood I couldn't see any type of hand holds. *How could anyone climb across this without using a pendulum?* Soon, I was hanging from the rope by my harness, then I began moving my feet on the smooth rock surface, first to my left until I couldn't go any further, then I ran back the opposite direction, gaining speed so I would soon be swinging. I began swinging like a kid, back and forth. On my last swing to the left I kept my feet moving in the direction of the ledge. As I came to the top of the swing, I reached up and grabbed the ledge with my left hand. Quickly, my right hand came across and also grabbed it. I pulled myself up, and was soon standing on a nice little ledge. It was actually wider than I had imagined, but still not a walking path. Hank instructed me to move over to where he was protected. The rock was flaked, hollow in the back, and made a perfect under-cling which I grasped as I walked along the ledge. I traversed over to Hank, and then clipped into the protection. When I was secure, I began belaying Hank further along the ledge. On occasion I would glance down. It was nearly straight down! It was incredible! *This had to be one of the greatest thrills of my life!*

Another lead ensued, and then we came to the second area where we would do a pendulum. This one was much easier, and seemed less exposed. It was still fun. Soon we found ourselves at the infamous **"Rotten Log."**

The log was longer than I had expected. It was leaning over a chasm, and the exposure was awesome. What's worse, the log definitely looked rotten, having a grayish color, smooth with no limbs. Yes, there were knobs where limbs used to be, but just bulging out enough to give a person problems if they decided to scoot up the log. It was just plain "freaky!" Thank God, Hank was going to do it first! I would just watch him closely and try to do the same thing.

"Is it better to scoot up it, or just try crouching low and climb up it with the hands on both sides of the log?" I asked.

Hank replied, "Whatever you feel better at doing. Put me on belay, and then watch how I do it. Hopefully, the log will last until we get across!"

What a thought! I was so concerned about how to climb up this steep thing, that I nearly forgot how rotten it was, and the possibility that it could break while we were on it. "Thanks a lot Hank for your encouragement!"

Hank crouched low, and began moving up the thirty to forty degree rotten plank, across a terrifying chasm; a void of approximately eight hundred feet. He moved smoothly, only hesitating when coming to the large knots. I remembered that Hank had been in gymnastics through his elementary and high school years, and I was sure that it was helping him to balance now at this awkward angle. Although I usually had good balance in other sports, I was lousy in gymnastics, so I decided then and there that when it was my turn I would sit on that log, and shimmy myself up even if it took all day to do it.

Hank was soon at the other side of the chasm. He climbed off the log onto the rocks, and began setting up a belay on the other side. I was thinking that this had better be the end of the scary stuff, because I don't know if I can handle much more. I was again brought back to reality with the familiar, "**On Belay!**"

I moved over to the log, sitting down on it with my legs on both sides. Wow! This log was leaning at a steep angle! I tried sliding up it. I could barely move, and it hurt my rear-end. I continued to try to move up it, but it was slow and physically demanding. Soon, the sweat was pouring down my face. I reached the first knob, grabbed around it hoping that it would help me, but it didn't. I was quickly becoming exhausted, and at this rate I would never make it up to the top.

"Hank, I'm going to try to stand on it, and do it your way."

I heard him reply, "O.K. Go for it. I have you on a good belay."

Now, how to stand up? If my balance is not good, or a foot slips off, I am looking down eight hundred feet. Even though I was on a good belay, any fall would be disastrous, resulting in crashing into the rock on the other side of the chasm and probably causing major injuries. I didn't relish the idea of hanging badly injured eight hundred feet above the valley floor. The adrenaline was really pumping now! I quickly put that thought out of my mind and concentrated on my next move. I placed my hands further ahead of me, and then pulled myself up with my knees on the log. Boy, did I feel unstable at this time! Slowly, I pushed myself up onto my feet, still crouching very low, and with my hands holding onto both sides of the log. I was up! Now, can I move upward? I moved very slowly at first, concentrating on my balance, and found that it wasn't too bad. Putting my concentration totally on the log beneath me and avoiding looking at the void below me, I began moving up the log in a faster motion. I was actually moving up this beast! Before long I was across the chasm, and climbing down to the firm rock below me. I let out a "Whew! Thank you Lord!"

"Well, we don't have to worry about that log anymore." Hank added, "Come to think of it, it may not even be here next year at this time." (Note- it fell three years later.)

I replied, "To tell you the truth, I don't believe I will be here to find out if it is or not." I knew that I would never climb this route again, and so I didn't have to worry about being on it when it collapsed. Deep down, I hoped that it would be around for a few years so that others could enjoy the same thrill as I had, but I knew that the condition of the old rotten log would not allow it to last forever. The rough winter months would probably destroy it soon.

Soon, we were climbing again. The climbing was now very enjoyable, and I knew that there were only a few more rope lengths before we came to a broad smooth wall (expansive slab) which was two hundred feet across and I guessed had to be climbed using only friction. I was certain that it couldn't be too bad, especially after what we had already done. With all my concentration on the climbing I hadn't noticed the clouds that were building up above us. They had a dark and ominous look to them. The clouds had made it a little cooler, which helped with the tremendous thirst that I was experiencing. As I approached the end of the last pitch, just opposite the friction slab, I heard Hank above me mention something about the weather not looking too good.

Hank was settled in a good belay spot among some small rocks just a short distance to the right of the expansive slab.

"Hank, what do you think about those clouds?" I asked as I came up to him.

"I think we are going to get some rain. We need to get you set up here quickly so I can get across this thing before it does. I sure don't want to be trapped up here!"

The thought of being trapped up this high was not very pleasant. We only had a couple of hours of daylight left. With rain and darkness, it would mean spending the night crouched next to this wall, exposed to whatever nature had in store for us, including lightning.

I quickly moved up to Hank, clipped into the protection, and then went about putting Hank on belay. "That wall looks awfully smooth. Is there anything to hold onto out there?"

"It's mainly a friction climb. Just keep your hands flat on the rock." Hank added, "There is no ledge to walk on, so we'll have to use the friction of our rock shoes. I believe it is around 200 ft. across, so, I'll traverse over to where there should be some kind of bolt to use for protection. If I remember correctly, it is more than half way across. I'll then bring you over to that spot, and then we'll belay the rest of the way to the trees."

Looking at the smooth wall across from us, I could see how it was steeply sloped, then dropped off straight down, just a couple of yards below where we would cross. Again, I thought of all the bad possibilities and my stomach began to churn again. This would be another new experience for me. The only other long friction pitch I had climbed was earlier that day, far below, where I had nearly slipped off the rock.

These thoughts were running through my mind as Hank prepared to begin his climbing. It was just a few yards to our left, and then he would be on the friction slab. Just as he began moving, I felt the first drops of rain. **"Hank, its' beginning to sprinkle!"** I said with alarm in my voice.

Hank quickly replied, "I felt it also. It's going to get slick. I've got to at least get over to that belay point before it gets worse! I'm heading out. Wish me luck!"

Hank moved swiftly, and soon was using friction to traverse across the wall. I watched intently, making sure that I could stop him in case he slipped off the steep slope. As I let the rope out, I thought to myself that for each foot that he moves across, it is one more foot that he will fall if he slips off, and I had better be well prepared for a very forceful pull on the rope. *Just don't fall*, I thought to myself.

Within fifteen minutes or so he was two-thirds the way across. He began attaching himself to some sort of protection in the rock. Then it began! The rain started coming down in large drops, at first lightly, and then building into a downpour. 'Holy Moly!' How are we ever going to get across now? I could just imagine us trapped at 1,300 feet overnight, with me, sitting in the rocks and Hank standing alone on the slab, over a hundred feet away, totally exposed to the elements.

Hank yelled across to me, "Gary, you've got to get yourself across to where I am, so we can get off this thing!"

I replied, "I can try, but I don't think it will work!" The rain was now beginning to run down the rock in little streams. "Am I on belay? I'll try and see what happens."

"You're on belay. Go for it, but be careful," Hank yelled back.

I began moving out of my tiny belay spot towards the sloped slab of rock. I could feel the rope tension between Hank and I, but I thought to myself, it would do little good if I fall. Soon I was at the smooth, sloped slab. I turned toward the wall, placing my hands on it. I then placed my left foot against the smooth surface. **My foot slid off as if on butter!** I tried again, but again the same results. The water was now running down my hands and arms, and I was getting soaked. I yelled, "Hank, it won't work. It's too damn slick!"

"You've got to get across to me!" Hank yelled back.

What a situation to be in! I knew that I needed to get over to him because he would never be able to get back to me, but I knew it was impossible. I would slip off just trying, and there I would be, hanging, and possibly unconscious much higher than the Empire State Building. What would we do then? No way! It wasn't worth taking the chance. I began praying, asking the Lord for help. *Dear Lord, you must show me the way.*

I looked around me. Slightly back, and up above, there appeared to be a fairly good crack system. It went up around thirty feet to what looked like a possible ledge that ran horizontal along the smooth wall. It seemed to go about midway of the wall, and then disappeared. Just below where the ledge disappeared was a small tree growing out of the rock. Possibly, if I could climb the crack to the ledge above, and if the ledge was climbable, I could traverse across and above the small tree. If I could climb down to the tree, Hank could then allow the rope to swing over the tree, and then we could figure out something the rest of the way. I yelled over to Hank, telling him my thoughts.

"Gary, if you could do it, get over there to the tree, possibly you could pendulum off the tree over to me."

"Hank, I'm going to try it. Wish me luck!" I then moved back a few steps to a point where I could get my fingers into the crack system, and started climbing upward. It wasn't difficult climbing, and I soon found myself coming to the ledge. *Now, if only the ledge is large enough!*

With anticipation, I reached up and placed my hand on the ledge and began pulling myself up. The ledge was just large enough for me to get my body onto. '**Thank you Lord**', I said to myself. I shuffled across the ledge on my knees, being very careful not to fall. I felt safe climbing up the cracks, but this was different, as I didn't have anything to grasp. I inched myself along and finally came to the point above the tree where the ledge disappeared. This was amazing! It was though God had put the tree just below where the ledge ended, knowing that we would need it someday.

Now, how to get down to the tree? It wasn't far below, possibly ten to fifteen feet, and there seemed to be some thin holds to grasp onto. I lowered myself from the ledge, finding the tiny but adequate hand holds. I came to the tree, which seemed to be pretty sturdy. I climbed down the opposite side of the tree, so that the rope ran under and then around it, giving me adequate friction.

"Hank, I'm going to lower myself. Keep the rope snug." With one hand on the tree, and the rope lying across the strongest part of the tree near where it came out of the rock, I lowered myself until I was hanging. Here I was, hanging from a rope slung over a tree growing out of a rock wall!

"You're doing great Metternich!" Hank yelled with a more confident tone in his voice. I'll lower you a few more yards, until you have enough rope to do a pendulum over to me."

Hank must have been forty to fifty feet further across from me, so he would need to lower me down at least that far so that the rope would reach him when I did the pendulum. Down and down he lowered me. I was nearly at the bottom of the bulging rock, at the point where it dropped straight off, before we had enough rope. It was an eerie feeling hanging just above the 1,300 foot void.

Hank yelled, "I think that will do it! Go ahead and start your pendulum."

I looked up. Far above me I could see the rope around the small tree. It still looked safe. I whispered a little prayer, and then began stepping towards my left with my feet flat against the rock. The rain had slowed down to a sprinkle, but the water was still running down the glass-like rock. Occasionally my feet would slip, but I continued to build up momentum, first running to my left, then to the right. On my third swing to the left I gained enough momentum to reach Hank and the small ledge he was standing on. As I gained the ledge, he grabbed a hold of me, and I ended up standing next to him, facing inward towards the rock.

"Here I am my friend. Now what do we do?" I asked. It was funny, but not enough to laugh. We were both standing on a ledge that was only a few inches wide. While he was clipping me into the protection, I was amazed to see that the bolt that he was using for protection was broken off and only a few inches long, and that he had wrapped a small piece of webbing around it, tying a knot on the end to prevent it from slipping off. I then added, "You actually belayed me with that as the anchor?"

Hank answered, "It was all I had. But it worked, didn't' it?

Yes it did, I thought. ***Now I knew that the decision not to try traversing across was the proper one. A fall could have been deadly.*** "Yes Hank, I'm glad that I'm here."

"Now, somehow we've got to get the rest of the way across this wall and into the trees. Do you think you can traverse across?" Hank asked.

It was still wet and slick, and I answered immediately, "I don't think so."

Hank then unclipped my rope from my harness, and proceeded to pull the rope over the tree limb and to where we were standing. Soon the end of the rope was in our possession.

This whole thing seemed so ludicrous to me. Here I am, standing on that narrow ledge, thirteen hundred feet high, secured onto a broken bolt, and with dark looming clouds above us. We had completed so much of our objective, and with only a small distance to go our lives still hung in the balance. A mistake here could negate everything we had accomplished to this point. Maybe it was because of what we had already been through, or possibly the fuzziness in my head caused by dehydration and exhaustion, but I felt no fear. More than that, I think I felt peace, knowing that God had brought us this far, and he would not fail us now. I also trusted Hank, feeling that he would figure something out. Another positive sign, the sprinkles of rain had stopped, and the rock was actually drying out.

Hank then came up with an idea, "I think I'll have you rappel down a short way off this anchor, then a short pendulum over into the trees. What do you think?"

I looked down. I had never rappelled at such a high elevation, but I felt confidence in my ability in doing it. I was concerned about the anchor, since I would be hanging from a runner wrapped around a broken bolt. All it had to do was to slip off the end and we would both be gone. "Let's do it Hank and get it over with! I want to get off this darn ledge!"

"O.K. my friend. When you rappel, go real easy. No hot-dogging!"

"Don't worry Hank. No hot dogging, and I'll go as slow and as smooth as I possibly can. Just keep that runner from sliding off the end of the bolt. O.K?"

I slipped the rope through my figure eight, and clipped into the harness, grasping the rope coming off the anchor with my left hand. I began letting the rope slip through my right hand, sitting back into my harness, spreading my legs and allowing the bottom of my shoes to guide me down the smooth rock. Slowly I moved downward. I knew that Hank had his fingers pressed tightly against the end of the bolt to prevent the runner from slipping off.

After I descended twenty to thirty feet below the ledge, Hank yelled and told me that he thought it was far enough. Then he told me to start my pendulum. Again, very gently, I began moving back and forth. It wasn't far to the trees, and I soon grabbed the edge of the rock, climbed over the side and stepped onto the ground.

What a feeling! I was on **"terra firma."** I quickly moved up to a large tree, unclipped the rope and tied it around the tree. Now, Hank had a secure anchor to come scooting across on. I then got on my hands and knees and kissed the ground. I was alive and well, and so happy.

Hank quickly traversed across to me, using the firmly attached rope. We gave each other a big hug before sitting down, almost totally spent. We sat there a few minutes, catching our breath and looking back across at what we had traversed. I had such a great feeling of accomplishment.

This had to be the toughest thing that I had ever done!

Our throats were parched. Having run out of water hours before, I was about as thirsty as I could remember. We could hear water running somewhere above us. Getting on our feet, we scrambled up through the dirt a short distance and amazingly found water running down a limb from a leaning tree.

"Is that water okay to drink?" I asked.

"Probably not! It could have Giardia or other parasites in it" Hank answered back. "Could make us sicker than dogs!"

"You know Hank, I don't really care. I'll deal with that later. Right now I'm just too thirsty." Without hesitating, I quickly retrieved one of my empty plastic water bottles out of my pack and began filling it up. The water was running down the limb fast enough that it took only a minute to fill my bottle up. I lifted the bottle and quickly drank the whole thing. It felt so soothing to my burning throat! I filled the water bottle again. Again, I quickly drank the whole thing. It was 'heavenly,' and at that point of time, nothing could have replaced the great pleasure of quenching my thirst. Hank decided to do the same. We drank water until we couldn't drink anymore. Then we filled our bottles one more time and replaced them in our packs.

It was beginning to get dark, and knowing that we still had a long way back, we quickly put on our packs, and scrambled up through the trees and brush to the top of the wall. Our route was to take the steep trail down the North Dome Gully, but first we had to traverse below the great Arches. To do this we had to pass underneath the North Dome, a strange looking mountain that looked like an Old Prussian helmet. The lower slopes of North Dome were slanted polished granite, still very slick from the rain. This was another area that we had to be very careful not to slip on. Across the valley I could still make out Half Dome, one of the giant granite rocks of Yosemite.

It seemed that the traverse would never end, but finally we came to the area where we needed to find the trail down the steep gully. This gully is used as a descent route for climbers, but it is very steep and exposed. Many a climber in the past had completed a climb, and then lost their life trying to descend this gully. Finding the route down in the growing darkness was our biggest problem, and we had to be extremely careful. A few times we got off course and found ourselves looking over some cliff, then back peddling to find the proper route. Some of the descent was so steep that we actually sat down and slid on our rear ends down the loose, muddy scree, grabbing at small bushes to slow us and avoid being out of control.

Finally, a couple of hours later we came to the bottom of the route, then bush whacked through brush and small trees until we came to one of the park's paved roads. Thank goodness we were down and safe! Now, all we had to do was hike the mile or so back to the parking lot where the car was parked.

We reached the car around nine p.m. Hank's little V.W. Bug was still parked there, and amazingly there was no parking ticket. There were many cars parked in the lot now, probably belonging to those having drinks or dinner at the Ahwahnee Lodge. It didn't take long after reaching the car to throw off our packs, and quickly open the cooler in the car containing the ice cold Rainier Ale. Popping the lids, we then sat on the bumper of the car, and began guzzling the ale, and reminiscing about the day's events. Our bodies were spent, but we were elated at achieving our climb, especially under the circumstances, first the heat, then the rain showers. The guidebook talks about many climbers on this route spending the night bivouac'd overnight at the top of the route because of running out of time, but we had made it back.

A white Lincoln Town car pulled up, parking near us. The man, a "Colonel Sanders" looking type of gentleman, all dressed in white, with his lady, also dressed in white got out of their car and stared at us. We must have been a **sight** to them. We were still soaking wet, with clothes covered with dirt from sliding down the gully, and me with blood smeared all over my pants. They both turned their noses into the air, and walked off towards the lodge.

"Hank, I don't think they appreciated us being here. They would never realize that you are a doctor, and I am a CPA, and not just two grubby climbers." Sometimes, it is hard to respect people who have their noses out of joint, just because they have money and wear beautiful clothes.

Hank laughed, and then added, "You know Gary, I wouldn't trade my life for theirs at any price."

****

Mark was still waiting for us at my pickup. He looked a little worried, but as we drove up and he recognized the vehicle a look of relief filled his face, then he gave us a big smile.

"Dad, did you make it?"

"We sure did, Mark. You can tell by my hands and clothes that it was a tough one, at least for me. We got poured on just before the end of the climb, causing us some anxiety, but we worked things out, and we're here. I could tell that Mark was anxious to tell me about his experiences, so I asked, "How was your day?"

"Well, I spent most of the day hiking around, and riding through the park on busses. An amazing thing happened when I was riding one of the busses. There were three climbers on the bus, two guys and a girl. They were all dirty and tired, and one guy looked like you Dad, with blood on his clothes. I noticed his hands were pretty torn up. I asked them if they had climbed, and they told me that they just completed Royal Arches. I told them that my Dad was on that climb, and asked if they had seen you and Hank. They said that they had watched you coming up, way below them. Probably a couple of hours behind."

He hesitated for a moment and then related what had happened that day. "Dad, I've got to tell you about the miracle! His voice was very excited now. "You told me not to leave the keys in the pickup, right? Well, I accidentally locked them in. I felt so bad, and after unsuccessfully trying to get them out, I left for the day. When I returned I was so worried, thinking that you would be mad at me. Earlier, I had gotten into the canopy with no effort, but found that the back window was locked. I again climbed into the canopy to rest. I sat there a few minutes, looked at the window, and then decided to try opening it gain. It was locked for sure! I just sat there sort of depressed. I then prayed, "Dear God, I need your help to open this thing!" I waited for a moment, and then tried it again. This time the window opened! Dad, it was a miracle!"

I could see the joy on his face, the joy of experiencing God answering his prayer. I too had experienced God answering my prayers that day, but I would wait until later to tell him about it, as I would not take this **moment** from him.

CHAPTER VI

POPO

Explosions! All around us, booming explosions! Was this a dream? Was I dreaming of combat? The tent was lighting up as if the sun was shining, but it was the middle of the night! Silence and darkness for a few seconds, then another explosion! They were so close!

I sat up quickly, shaking my head, trying at the utmost to come out of my dream world. Within seconds, I realized that this was not part of a dream. This was really happening! Then, I remembered that we were camped high on the western side of Mt. Rainier, just below the Sunset Amphitheater, a sheer wall of rock and ice. We were in the midst of the worse lightning storm I had ever experienced!

Our group consisted of five climbers, nestled in three tents at the 9,500 ft. level of the mountain. We were camped on ice, on an outcrop of rock, totally exposed to the elements, and within a few feet of a thousand foot drop off to the glacier below. It was a precarious situation in the least. Being in the middle of the night, there was no escape. When we realized what was happening, we shouted back and forth, and decided to stay low until the storm passed. It was just a matter of continuing to lay in our sleeping bags, hoping and praying for the best.

A couple of days earlier, we had been excited at the aspects of this classic climb up the "Cycle Route" of the Tahoma Glacier. The weather forecast was favorable, and with a strong group of climbers, we were confident that this would be a memorable climb. On the first day, we had made our way up to our first camp at over 7,000 ft., an elevation gain of 5,400 feet. Our campsite at Tookaloo Spire was very impressive, with a tremendous view of the whole west side of the mountain the Indians called "Tahoma". It was exhilarating to be at this site, and on this side of the great mountain. No other climbers were there. Just us!

Once our camp was set up, we lit the climbing stoves, boiling water, and began eating our freeze-dried dinners. As the sun began to set, the alpenglow on the west flanks of Rainier was spectacular. But to our surprise, we viewed higher on the mountain an ominous formation of lenticular clouds settling on the summit. We stared in disbelief, knowing that this type of cloud was a forecaster of bad weather. It wasn't just a normal cloud cap, but others followed and they were stacking, one on top of the other. The mood in our group soon turned solemn. Some in the group tried to laugh it off, but we all knew deep down that this was a warning that you can't ignore.

I was the designated leader of this group of five guys. Early in the winter, me, and two of the climbers, Mark and Steve, had agreed to use this climb as training for a trip to Mexico to climb a couple of the high volcanoes later in the year. I had climbed this route ten or eleven years earlier, and knew that it would test you both physically and mentally. Mt. Rainier at an altitude of 14,411 ft. is a good stepping-stone to the seventeen and eighteen thousand foot volcanoes. Now, as I lay there listening to the lightning strikes hitting the mountain and the sound ricocheting all around us, the last thing on my mind was a trip to sunny Mexico. At this moment, I just wanted to survive. If I could have gotten out of my tent and run to safety, I surely would have, but knowing that lightening generally strikes the highest exposed objects, it was silly to even try. We would be great targets on the exposed ground. As I lay there, I wondered what it would be like to be hit by lightning.

In the next tent, close enough that it was touching mine were Steve and Pete. Steve Autio was a good climbing friend. We had been on several good climbs together in the past. He was very strong, and had good technical skills. One of his assets was a great sense of humor. While trudging up a mountain, Steve could keep you in stitches telling jokes and wise cracking. He, as well as the other climbers in our group were silent at this time, probably doing what I was doing, praying. The lightning continued to strike the steep walls of the mountain, when suddenly, out of this violent and noisy environment, Steve shouted, "Dear Lord, if you will save me, I promise that I will quit drinking!" Normally this would have been very funny, and would have cracked me up, but we were not in a funny situation. I'm not sure whether he meant it to be a joke, or if he was serious, but it was said.

We lay there for hours, listening to nature's force pounding the mountain, and then sometime during the night it quit. The wind blew, and the sleet and snow came down, but I soon went into a deep sleep. I awoke as the first dawn of light lit the mountain. I could hear the others stirring also. It was still storming, but we quickly got out of our bags, broke camp, and headed down the windy, snowy, cold mountain.

****

As we drove in our rented Volkswagen Kombi Van from Mexico City toward our day's destination, the small town of Amecameca, I half dozed, occasionally staring out at the dry arid country that was such a contrast to what we had left in Oregon. It was October, and we had left the state of Oregon during the typical rainy fall weather. We had planned on spending three nights in Mexico City, trying to acclimatize at an altitude that was 7,000 ft. higher than where we lived. The next day, for something to do, we explored some of the sights of Mexico City, and managed to climb two of the major Aztec pyramids for exercise. We also stocked up on our provisions, which included an ample supply of rum. During our first evening in the hotel room, as everyone was sampling the spirits that we purchased, I thought about what Steve had blurted out while in the storm on Rainier. I had a notion to remind Steve of his promise to God, but not wanting to sound judgmental, I decided to remain quiet.

After only two nights in Mexico City we felt we just couldn't take the polluted air anymore so we decided to leave a day early for our trip south to the volcanoes. We packed up, and headed out early the next morning.

Driving in Mexico is a daring undertaking. I was glad that Bill Brownlee was driving. A big lanky red head, Bill was as stubborn and persistent as the Mexican drivers. Just getting out of the city was a harrowing experience. With several lanes of autos all trying to nose ahead of one another, it took guts and a good horn to maneuver through it. Bill added to that a lot of swearing and yelling, but succeeded in getting us outside the city and into the countryside. Not only are the traffic and roads bad in Mexico, but in addition, you have the fear of being robbed by bandits, or shaken down by unscrupulous law enforcement people. We had been advised by others who had made trips to Mexico not to get into trouble with the police. Don't even get into a traffic accident. They lock you up, and then ask questions. The police are notorious for asking for some kind of pay off, whether you commit an offense or not.

As we got onto the toll highway, we could see a line of traffic in front of us. There was some type of officers collecting tolls ahead of us. We could see that they were certainly taking their time about it. As we were finally inching up to the tollbooth, we could see a police officer giving the driver in front of us a tough time. After a few minutes of abuse, the driver pulled out a wad of money and handed it to the officer, and was then allowed to go on. Bill commented, "I'll be damned if we are going to give that guy any of our cash." Looking around, we noticed that there didn't seem to be any police vehicles standing by. Bill continued, "I don't see any police vehicles. What about running it?"

I didn't know about the others, but I certainly didn't like what I was hearing and was about to say something, but just as we were slowing down to stop at the designated stopping area, Bill suddenly hit the throttle. The V.W. sputtered, then roared, and off we went. The officer just looked at us stunned at first, but then he ran after us, waiving and yelling!

"Bill, what the heck are you doing?" We all took turns voicing our concerns. "They'll throw us in jail and toss the keys away!"

Bill responded in a calm tone, "Na! We don't have to worry, they didn't even have freak'n radios!" Then we all began laughing. What we had done was so ridiculous that it was funny.

That was the end of my relaxation and daydreaming. The rest of the drive to Amecameca was spent watching out for some type of patrol car or motorcycle with its sirens on, or possibly a roadblock. I could see the headlines, **"Five grubby, drug running Americana's shot during get away on toll road."**

Not only were we concerned by our escape, but the clouds were beginning to come in, and a few sprinkles of rain were starting to splatter our windshield. Great! We leave the rainy northwest and come to the desert country of Mexico only to find that the rain had followed us here also!

As we arrived in Amecameca, the rain was coming down so hard that we could hardly see. Fortunately we were able to find the motel called the "Popo" where a group of us had stayed two years earlier. Since this was the off-season, the room rates were very reasonable; around five dollars per night each, plus they had a restaurant where we could get our dinner for the night, as well as a decent breakfast the following morning. Not too bad for a group of grubby climbers. We quickly went to our rooms, stowed our bags and gear, and then headed for the restaurant to satisfy our burning appetites, since we hadn't eaten all day.

We had a dinner of pollo (chicken), soup and of course refried beans, washed down with the local cervesa. It was delicious, and we soon felt like human beings again. After doing our planning for the next day, we headed for our rooms, hoping to get a good night's sleep. Our plans were to arise early, do some shopping in the local market for extra food, then to drive up to the lodge for our first climbing destination, Mt. Popocatepetl. After taking a chilly cold shower, I soon was in bed, hoping to be fast asleep. My roommate was Mark Bovee, whom I hadn't known for a long time, but was friendly and easy to get along with. We chatted for a while, and then turned out the lights. I lay there thinking about the day's events, and glad that we have made it this far. The weather still seemed to be a concern, but we'd just have to hope for an opening, and go for it. Soon I was fast asleep.

****

We arose around six in the morning. I could hear roosters crowing, which was probably a good sign, indicating that the weather was not too bad. It was chilly in our room, but soon we were dressed, and headed over to our friend's room. Gathering our friends, we then headed for breakfast. Soon, we were chowing down on bacon and eggs, and refried beans. The only thing missing was good coffee. I had brought some good premium coffee with me, but we would have to wait until we were able to fire up our stoves and heat water, which would be after we had picked up some fuel and arrived at base camp.

The market was typically mobbed by people, pushing and shoving to get to the best food at the best prices. We felt conspicuous, since we were the only **"gringos"** there, but we tried to blend in with the rest of the swarm as much as we could and search our food needs. I had warned the others not to attempt to take pictures because it created contempt by the locals. Even without taking pictures, we seemed to get glares from some of the populace, but in general the people were friendly and only intent on selling their goods. After buying a large bag of bread rolls, fresh carrots, tomatoes and some fruit, we quickly exited the busy market. We found white gas at a station near the market, and felt relieved that we would be able to use our stoves on the mountain.

Soon we were back at the van, had it loaded and were ready to go. Still our designated driver, Bill Brownlee hopped into the driver's seat, and turned the key. Nothing happened! The battery was dead.

"Looks like the beginning of another great day," someone commented. "Well, let's get out and push this thing." Three of us jumped out and began pushing the van so that Bill could start it with the rolling momentum. "Ka chug, ka chug," sounded the engine, but it wouldn't start. "Let us get it going faster before you try to start it Bill," I gasped, as we pushed in the thin air. We pushed as fast as we could, and when the vehicle was moving about as fast as it was going to, it suddenly leapt to life! We were on our way!

As we left Amecameca for our drive of approximately eighteen mile to Tlamacas, at the foot of Popo, the clouds began to thin out, and every few minutes we would get a glimpse of part of the great mountain. The road was curvy the next fourteen miles, but we soon reached Corte's Pass, which is at the elevation of 12,000 ft. It is here that the Spanish invader Cortes crossed the mountains with his army centuries earlier. This pass is set between the two great mountains: Popocatepetl on the south and Iztaccihuatl (Ixty) on the north. There is a monument at the junction turning towards Popo, of the Spaniard Cortes. I'm not sure why they have one because according to history he was a murdering, plundering individual who only wanted to conquer the people and reap in the treasures of the country. After a couple of more miles we reached our destination of Tlamacas, located at 12,950 ft. There is a climbing lodge located here where you can rent bunks for a couple of nights alleviating the need to sleep outdoors in tents, and from where you can begin the ascent of the mountain.

It seems to be a strange place for a lodge, but during the busy seasons of the year it is quite crowded with visitors trying to escape the heat and get a good view of the mountain. Since it is located at such a high altitude there are many stories about the tourists and the maladies they suffer. Many come here just to party. Tequila and altitude don't mix, and some have gone home with worse than a hangover. Also, because access to the mountain is so near, many deaths have occurred on the mountain by ill prepared hikers, dying because of either the altitude or from the fierce storms that come up. The mountain is strewn with crosses and ornaments as monuments to those that have perished on the mountain. However, many are merely monuments for deceased family or loved ones, placed there by a hiking friend or relative.

With the summit at an elevation of 17,887 ft., and the lodge at 12,950 ft., the elevation gain of 4,900 ft. can be accomplished in one day. Without proper acclimatization, the results can be deadly. Even after spending a couple of nights at the lodge, the body is not properly acclimated. I recall talking to some experienced climbers that after spending two nights at the lodge they still experienced throwing up blood, and bleeding from the ears as they neared the summit. On the positive side is that you are quickly up and quickly down before any edema sets in. So, anyone getting sick high up on the mountain may be able to be brought down to lower elevations before the edema becomes deadly. The only cure is to reach lower elevations quickly. With my years of climbing, I've come to the conclusion that it is better that mountains not have such easy access, in order to keep the inexperienced people off of them. Normally, inexperienced people will not put forth any great effort to reach a mountain, such as hiking a considerable distance while carrying a heavy pack.

Being Monday morning, the lodge was fairly empty. If you are a climber, you are given special treatment, because they never know whether you are a famous world-class climber, or not. Many famous climbers have visited this lodge and climbed Popo, such as Reinhold Messner and others. We were well received in the lobby by the friendly employees and had no trouble renting our bunk spaces for the next couple of nights. As we walked into the bunk type rooms, we seemed to be the only ones there. It was a nice feeling that we would not be sharing our room with a bunch of other climbers. The forecast of poor weather could have been the reason for the lack of occupants.

Once we had picked our bunks and had put our gear away, I suggested that we get out our small climbing packs, load them with adequate warm gear and a few snacks, and take a hike up the mountain for exercise. I had noticed that the others seemed to be doing very well with the altitude, and I was hoping we could go up to at least 14,000 ft. today in order to help us acclimate a little more. It would be a good test for us, as well as help getting the travel kinks out of our bodies. Everyone seemed enthusiastic about hiking some distance up the mountain to see what it was like.

****

It was foggy and moist as we made our way up the well-trodden path leading up from the lodge. I remembered from my previous trip here that there was a fork in the path a short ways up from the lodge. We would need to stay to the right, virtually ascending straight up the mountain. The path was dirt and rocks, with no snow. Our lungs were working

160

hard to bring in as much oxygen as possible at this high altitude. Even though we couldn't see anything through the fog, it felt good to be exerting our bodies, moving again up a mountain.

"We need to go up into those rocks," I called out, "And keep traversing this side of the ridge."

We were on the northwest side of the mountain, and following a route named the Ventorrillo. If we were on course, this route would take us up to an old hut located at 14,632 ft., named the Queretano hut. This was my planned goal for the day. It was now about two in the afternoon. At the speed we were moving, it would take us less than two hours to get there, and then less than an hour to get back to the lodge. We should have plenty of time for rest this evening.

"How's everyone feeling?" I asked. Each one responded that they were doing great! "Any headaches?"

No one responded affirmative, so that was a very good sign. Headaches are usually one of the earlier signs of altitude sickness. This mountain would be our first test for strength and the effects of high altitude climbing. This was the fifth highest mountain in North America, but our next goal would require traveling southeast to Pico Orizaba, the third highest mountain in North America at 18,700 ft. I felt confident that we had the right group of climbers for this trip.

An hour or so later, we reached the end of our destination for the day, the Queretano hut. We were now 221 ft. higher than Mt. Rainier in Washington.

"It's break time! Let's take some time here, and then we'll head down. It looks like there is some clearing off to the north."

You could just make out the lodge far below, and then across the valley you could see Mt. Iztaccihuatl, with an altitude of 17,342 ft. This mountain was called the **"Sleeping Lady"** because from a distance it looks like a woman laying down facing the sky. I had climbed this mountain two years earlier, but it wasn't on our schedule this trip.

"Hey Metternich, is that a difficult climb? Asked Steve.

"It's tougher than this one, and there can be some very hard steep ice even on the easier routes" I responded. "It's also a very long day, because you have to travel over most of the long summit to reach the highest point. We had two people on our last trip that sat down and refused to go the final two hundred yards up to the summit because they were so exhausted."

"Hell, being that close I would have crawled if necessary to get to the summit," responded Bill.

"I know Bill, that's exactly what I told them. I'm not sure why they even came on the trip," I added.

"What's our plans for tomorrow?" asked Mark.

"I'm glad that you brought that up Mark. Since we are all doing so well on the altitude thing, I would like to shoot for the summit tomorrow. How's that sound?" Without waiting for an answer, I quickly added, "There are a couple of reasons for doing it tomorrow. First, if we get weathered off we still have one more day to climb it before leaving here for Orizaba. Secondly, if we make it, we will still have that extra day in dealing with Orizaba. I want to climb both of them, but Orizaba is my personal goal. I really think we can do this one with only one night of acclimating here."

Steve responded, "I'm all for it. Why don't we head down now, eat early, and try to get some good sack time?" Everyone agreed to go for it tomorrow.

Back at the lodge, we pulled out our climbing stoves, and food for the evening, and headed out to the foyer, a warm sheltered place, to heat our water and prepare dinner. It's hard to believe that they will let you fire up your stoves in the foyer, an enclosed entrance to the lodge, but they do. We soon had water boiling, adding it to our freeze-dried dinners.

As we ate the freeze-dried meals, we enjoyed with it the bread rolls and fresh vegetables that we had purchased at the market.
A fine bottle of wine would have topped it off, but we had no wine, and besides we didn't want to drink any alcohol before tackling the high altitude in the morning.

"What time are we getting up?" asked Bill.

"I was thinking around three a.m., and if we can get away at four thirty that should be sufficient. As strong as we are, I guess we'll be able to reach the summit in six or seven hours. I would like to summit before too many clouds come rolling in later in the morning. They seem to start gathering around ten or eleven." I added, "Hopefully we won't have any crevasse problems that could hold us up and waste valuable time."

We finished our dinner, cleaned up the foyer, and headed for our bunks. I finished packing a few items for the morning, and when I felt that I had done about all I could in preparing for the climb, I brushed my teeth and crawled into my nice warm sleeping bag.

****

As I lay there, my mind went back a couple of years to the previous trip down here. Since it was our first adventure to Mexico it was very exciting for me, and I believe for the others as well. There were six of us on this trip. I had talked my good friend and climbing partner Bob True into coming, even though he was hesitant at first. I think it was his wife and an issue of money that almost held him back, but I knew that he wanted to come so I pushed very hard. Three of the others I had climbed with a couple of times, Bill, Dallas and Mary, and the fourth person, Leslie, I had never met. Bill was a good guy who seemed to enjoy the outdoors. Dallas and Mary were a married couple that I could never seem to get in tune with. Leslie was a single girl, and I had heard a few stories about her wild side from some of my fellow climbers, but of course stories are stories! Four of us had flown from Portland, Oregon together, but Leslie met us in Los Angeles, since she had attended some "rock concert." My first impression of Leslie was not very good. She was a little plump, not looking in the best physical condition, and had this wild frizzy red hair. I probably was being a little judgmental, but I could imagine what her conditioning program had been. I had been assured by Dallas and Mary that Leslie would do all right, but I still had my doubts. Since this was a small type of expedition, costing money and time, I really expected everyone to be sincere about conditioning, and didn't want the trip to be ruined by all of us having to turn around at a crucial time during the climb because someone was out of shape. It was too late now. We'd just have to wait and see.

After arriving at base camp at Tlamacas, we spent the first night resting, and then took our conditioning hike the next day. The weather was beautiful and we had no problem finding the route up to the Queretano hut. Once we got there, Bob True and I felt fine, but the other three were having complications. All three had bad headaches, and one or two of them had upset stomachs. I was hoping that we would shoot for the summit the next morning and had told them my plans.

164

Bob said that was good with him, but the others seemed to be overly quiet about it.

After returning to the lodge later that afternoon, a couple of them commented that they were concerned about how they felt, and wondered about waiting another day. I suggested that they eat dinner, get a good a night's rest, and decide early in the morning. I told them that Bob and I would probably go even if they decided not to, since I was concerned that the weather might not hold very long. If that happened, then Bill who was experienced could lead the other two up the Las Cruces route, a much easier route than the Ventorrillo route that Bob and I had planned on climbing. Everyone seemed agreeable to this, and the three even seemed relieved. I knew that they had already made up their minds, and would not be going in the morning, but had decided to wake them anyway, just in case.

Bob and I had an enjoyable climb the next day. The route was in good condition, with the crevasses exposed enough that we could venture around them. It was sunny on the summit, and we enjoyed our breakfast at 17,887 ft., chatting and taking pictures of the beautiful scenery. We were back at the lodge by early evening.

The others seemed to be feeling better, and had decided to climb the next morning, doing the easier route as I had suggested. Bob and I had dinner in the foyer with them, telling them about the exciting day. Being pretty tired, we retired to our sleeping bags early. The others milled around a while getting prepared for the next morning, then also hit the sack for a few hours sleep, before having to arise in the early morning hours.

Each night, I thank my Father in heaven for the day's events, and pray for protection for my family and friends. As I lay there that night beginning to pray, the thought about praying for your enemies suddenly came into mind. Now, why was I thinking of that? Who were my enemies? I seemed to know who my friends were, but I wasn't so sure about my enemies. This thought persisted, and I couldn't seem to get it out of my mind. I know that I didn't feel very close to three people in our climbing group, but I wouldn't really consider them my enemies. On the other hand, I didn't have the same desire to pray for them as I did for example my children or close friends. I lay there for a long time wrestling with this. Eventually I went to sleep, but awoke after an hour or so, with this same thought in my mind. This time though, I sensed that I was being told to pray for all four of the other climbers. It certainly wasn't my desire to do so, but I did anyway. Sometimes I guess a person just needs to be obedient and follow their feelings. I seemed to need to do it. I prayed for their safety on the mountain, and asked forgiveness for my pride and being judgmental.

They were away around four in the morning, and we wished them a good climb as they left, then we went back to sleep. We got up in time to go to the little restaurant in the lodge and have bacon and eggs. We felt starved because of the previous days' exertion. That breakfast certainly tasted good! While we were there, a couple of other climbers, a man and his wife, who had just arrived came in. We introduced ourselves and started chatting, finding out that they were going to acclimate a couple of days, and then climb both Popo, and Ixty, which would be a day or two later than us. I mentioned that we had climbed Popo, and were planning also to do Ixty. The husband said that while his wife took a nap he wanted to drive over and scout out the road to Ixty. He had a rental vehicle, and invited us to go with him. Bob and I decided it was a good idea, but we also felt that one of us should remain at the lodge just in case there was an emergency having to do with our climbing group. Bob said that he was a little tired anyway, and recommended that I go.

The drive across the pass was an experience to say the least. There wasn't really a road, just tracks where vehicles had gone before. It was rough! It took us three or four hours to our destination and back. I was pretty tired by the time that I returned, but the trip was worth it, knowing that we would be able to find our way over there in a couple of days for our climb. I also got to know my friend pretty well. He was an emergency doctor from New Jersey, and had a lot of experience on climbing expeditions. We hit it off as friends, and I was hoping that he could accompany us on our Ixty climb, but it looked like they would be doing it a day or two after us. I would later find out that meeting this Doctor was not just a coincidence.

Bob and I had an early dinner, expecting our group to be back no later than six p.m. Six p.m. arrived and no sign of our people. It was now getting dark, and so around seven p.m. we decided to hike a ways up the mountain with our headlamps and possibly meet them on the trail. Hopefully they had not become lost. We trudged up the trail in the dark, this time turning to the left at the little junction where Bob and I had a day earlier climbed to the right. Our legs were still both stiff and weak from our previous' days climb, and we moved slowly. We would turn off our headlamps every few minutes, stop and look for some sign of flashlights coming in our direction. Still nothing!

We had been hiking for three quarters of an hour when we finally saw some lights coming. That must be them! As we got closer, we called out to them, and they responded. It was them! As we neared them we could see that it looked like someone was injured. Two members of the group were helping one of them to walk. As our lights finally lit up the faces we could see Dallas and Mary helping Leslie walk.

"What happened to you guys?" I asked.

"You wouldn't believe it!" Bill Saur responded. "Leslie slid down the mountain!"

"What do you mean, she slid down the mountain?" Bob asked.

"She lost control, as we rested close to the crater, she couldn't use her ice axe and slid all the way to the bottom." Bill answered.

"How bad is she hurt?" I asked, as both Bob and I moved quickly over to her, to see if we could help.

"She's pretty skinned up, but no broken bones," Dallas said. "Her ankles are pretty sore too!"

"Leslie, are you okay?" Bob asked.

"I think I'll survive, but it was close!" Leslie answered half sobbing. "I've torn the skin off my stomach, and arms, and it's awfully painful. I can walk but just need a little help."

Bob and I moved over to Leslie, "Here, we'll help you for a while," I offered.

Bob and I carefully grabbed Leslie under the arms on both sides and began helping her to continue towards the lodge. As we walked slowly on, the others filled us in on what happened. It had almost been a disaster! The party had reached the summit, and decided rather than take a break there, or on the dirt alongside of the crater rim, they opted to wait until they reached the top of their descent route on the snow. They had climbed down below the crater rim dirt, and sat down on the now hardening snow for their break. Even though the slope is only thirty degrees gradient, experienced climbers will normally drive in their ice axe, and attach the strap to their climbing belt in order to stop an accidental slip or fall. Apparently they had not thought of doing this. As they were sitting there eating snacks, Leslie suddenly started sliding! She grabbed her axe and tried to stop, but her speed and the hardness of the snow prevented her from digging it in. Faster and faster she went. The others just stood there helplessly, calling to her as she slid down the ice. Soon she disappeared into the clouds below.

As she raced down the steep slope, she flipped in the air several times, losing her ice axe, and eventually sliding approximately two thousand feet at a horrendous speed. Her body finally came to a stop, just a few feet from a pile of rocks. She had lost consciousness sliding down the mountain and she lay there a considerable time before she finally came to. There happened to be a couple of climbers at the bottom of the snowfield, near where she ended up, and they saw much of the fall. One of them fortunately was an E.M.T. (emergency medical technician) and was soon by her side, trying to comfort her and apply antiseptics to her wounds. They stayed with her until the other three showed up.

As I was listening to this story, someone showed me her crampons that she had been wearing. They were both broken and bent as if some rock had fallen on them. Crampons are made of a strong metal alloy and the force had to be spectacular to have damaged them this way

As we came close to the lodge, I left the four of them, and hurried down the trail to see if I could find my doctor friend. Luckily he was there, and available. As soon as we got Leslie into her room, the doctor examined her carefully.

"This is one fortunate young lady. No broken bones or internal injuries that I can determine. She is pretty badly bruised, and has lost a lot of skin on her arms and stomach. I would be a little concerned about infection. I'll cleanse her wounds, and apply more antiseptic, but tomorrow you might want to get her back to Mexico City to a hospital, or send her home on the earliest flight that you can find."

The next day Leslie tells us that she is doing all right, and that she doesn't want to ruin our climbing, and suggests that we take her to the Popo Motel where we had stayed earlier, and leave her there the next day as we climb Ixty. She really wanted to rest, and didn't feel up to driving back to Mexico City at this point anyway.

We took care of her that day, tending to her wounds, and allowing her to get plenty of rest. The next morning we arose at one-thirty a.m., and before leaving I asked her one more time if she would be all right. She said she would, and wished us a good climb.

Our climb the next day was successful, and when we returned late that night, we picked up Leslie, who seemed to be doing much better, and all of us went out and had some good Mexican food. Leslie was still hurting pretty bad, but wanted to go to Mexico City the next day with us, since our plans were to go there, then travel to Mazatlan the following day, spending a couple of days at the beach. She decided she would just play it by ear, deciding what to do once we reached Mexico City.

The next morning we all went to our little restaurant to have breakfast before heading out to Mexico City. For two days I had wanted to say something to Leslie. I wanted to tell her that it was a miracle of God that she survived the fall, but I never seemed to find the appropriate time. I didn't want to do it around the others, but so far we had never been alone. As we were eating breakfast, I reached into my pocket for something, and felt a small plastic bag with objects in it. It was two little Christian crosses that I had brought with me to give away. When traveling out of your country, it is a good idea to have some form of souvenirs with you to give away to special people that you meet on your journey. Not only does it help make friendships, but it promotes Goodwill among nations. At the last minute before leaving, I had grabbed these two crosses, putting them into the little plastic bag, and into my casual jacket. These crosses were special to me since I had gotten them in Israel the previous year on a tour to the Mideast, at the biblical site of Lazarus' tomb.

As we ate, I couldn't help but notice that Leslie had changed. Softness had replaced the hardness in her face. Even though not feeling well, there was sereneness, almost a wellness to her face. I knew what I needed to do. Now, all I needed was the time alone with her, and the courage to tell her. Once we had eaten, everyone just got up quickly and headed out of the restaurant to go finish packing. All of a sudden, it was just Leslie and I together. I said, "Leslie, I'll walk you back." We headed out of the restaurant. Once outside, I said to her, "Leslie, I need to say something to you."

She answered quietly, "Alright. What is it?" The tone in her voice was as if she knew that I had something important to tell her.

"You know Leslie, that was a miracle that you survived that fall, don't you?"

She responded with a quiet "Yes I do."

I went on, "Have you ever heard of Lazarus, from biblical times?"

Her answer was a quiet, "I'm not sure."

I continued, "Well, let me tell you about Lazarus. Lazarus and his two sisters, Mary and Martha were very close friends of Jesus. When Jesus was returning to Jerusalem from the Jordan River area, he was sent word that Lazarus was sick in bed in Bethany and was asked to come immediately to help Lazarus. Jesus, even though he loved Lazarus and his sisters chose to stay in the area he was in for another two days. When he finally arrived outside of Bethany, he was told that Lazarus had been dead for four days. The sisters were very distraught.

Mary who had gone out to meet Jesus was weeping and she told Jesus that if he had been there, Lazarus would have lived. Jesus was moved. He wept! He then asked where Lazarus was entombed, and asked to be taken to him. They took him there. A large crowd had gathered, some mourning Lazarus, and others to see this Jesus of Nazareth. Jesus prayed, and then ordered Lazarus to come out of the tomb. Lazarus soon came out, still covered with his burial clothes, but was alive."

I then reached into my pocket and took out the little cross. "Leslie, this cross is from Israel, and the tomb of Lazarus. I brought it to give to someone special, not knowing whom. I now know it was meant for you. God loves you very much! Like Lazarus, you were also dead, but you have been brought back from death and are now alive!"

I'm not sure where the words came from, but I said them. With tears in her eyes she thanked me. We hugged, and soon tears were streaming down both our eyes.

I am not sure what happened to Leslie after the trip. I do know that she quit climbing, was married about a year later, and was happy. I do know that both of us changed. I realized how I was so full of pride and judgmental, and only cared about the ones that I wanted to. I had learned a great lesson, one of loving my enemy. While these thoughts of the event that had taken place were still in my mind, I said my prayers for a safe climb for everyone, and quickly went to sleep.

****

The alarm rang at three a.m. Boy! I didn't even remember going to sleep. I quickly crawled out of the sleeping bag, slid into my climbing clothes and joined the others in the foyer for our early morning meal. After boiling water, I mixed the two packets of instant oatmeal with the water. Instant oatmeal doesn't taste that good at three-thirty in the morning, but I knew that I would need the energy, so I forced it down. I mixed my instant coffee next, and sipped on it as I finished preparing my gear for the climb. "Is everyone having fun?" I asked.

"You bet!" responded Steve. The others just moaned. "I guess someone's got to do it," added Steve.

We were right on time, heading out of the lodge at close to four-thirty a.m. It was still dark outside, but it wouldn't be too long before there would be light on the horizon. We turned on our headlamps and headed up the trail towards the mountain. The mountain was partially clear, as we could make out stars around the broken clouds. Maybe the weather would hold out for us. So far things looked good. The lights from our headlamps cast eerie shadows as we crunched our way up the trail towards the mountain. I felt strong this morning, probably better than I had for several days. It was probably the result of getting my system cleaned out of the dirty Mexico City air, and my lungs were now beginning to work properly.

Soon we came to our junction where the path cut to the left towards the Las Cruces route. We continued straight ahead, and were soon scrambling over small rocks and boulders on the trail. Hardly a word was said as we moved rapidly up the trail. At this time in the morning you just concentrate on getting into some kind of rhythm with your breathing while at the same time allowing your body to loosen up. Every once in a while I would stop and glance around to see if they were all close behind me. Good, we were all moving at the same speed.

As we arrived at the Queretano hut, the light was beginning to glow along the flanks of the mountain. Soon, it would be getting light enough to be able to turn our headlamps off. I stopped at the hut, "Let's take a quick water and snack break here." I found a rock to sit on, and then added, "Well, we're higher than Mt. Rainier again."

"Looks like we may have a good day for climbing," commented Bill. "Where does our trail go from here?"

"We'll head that direction," I answered, while pointing my light towards the southwest. "Our route sort of hugs the rock buttress on the right, and in another fifteen hundred feet we will be at the saddle and the next hut, which is located at around sixteen thousand feet. This is still a rock scramble, and we will be on these rocks all the way to the saddle."

"From here on, we will be setting an altitude record every step we take since none of us, except Metternich has been this high before," commented Steve. "Pretty darn exciting, I would say."

"Yep, and from here on is where the high altitude will really start getting to you, so keep deep breathing," I suggested.

After having a few sips of water, and downing some candy, gorp, etc., we slipped into our packs, and headed up the rocks. The short break was good, but bad in the sense that the legs didn't want to move yet, waiting for the flow of blood back into the muscles. Soon, we were moving at a good pace, ever higher and higher.

We were close to the glacier on our left, and could see the steep white ice, marked with many crevasses. I was grateful that we weren't getting on the glacier at this point, because of its' steepness. It should be less steep once we reached the saddle, and not as heavily crevassed. A cold breeze was beginning to pick up and seemed to be coming directly off the ice on our left. It stung the face, and I pulled the hood of my parka over my head, trying to stay warm. We were now on fairly steep rock, and began using our hands to support our movements. We were still moving at a good pace, stopping every few minutes to catch our breath.

The terrain was beginning to round in front of us, with the glacier showing less steepness. It had been about an hour and a half since we had left the last hut, and I thought that I could just about make out the next hut at the saddle not too far from us. As we moved over and around some of the last remaining boulders, suddenly in front of us was the Teopixcalco hut, settled next to some huge rocks. We were at the saddle! From here, we would take our last break, rope up, and then head up the glacier towards the summit.

"We're at the saddle guys! From here, it's straight up that glacier to the summit," I exclaimed cheerfully.

"Thank God!" Steve answered. "It will be nice to get onto the snow for a change. This rock scrambling is tiring."

The wind was whipping around, and it was quite cold. We all put on some additional clothing, and then took our morning breakfast break. Each guy pulled out anything that would appeal to him at that altitude, since food begins to taste lousy the higher you climb. We all knew that we would need the energy, so we forced ourselves to eat something. Also, dehydration can set in very fast at high altitudes, so we began replacing the precious liquids to our bodies, forcing ourselves to drink the ice-cold water.

The mountain was lit up by now, except we were still in the shade, being on the northwest side of the mountain. It would have been nice having some sunshine on us to warm our bodies but it would have to wait. The mountain was mostly visible, but some clouds were beginning to pour down from the summit. It didn't look too ominous, so we set about getting on our harnesses, crampons, and laying out the rope.

After about ten minutes we were ready to tie ourselves into the rope. When at last we were secured to the rope, we began moving up the mountain. It hadn't been a long break, but we were better off moving and staying warm, rather than sitting around getting cold.

The glacier was very firm, and you could hear the crunch as our crampons bit into the ice. I headed up in the direction that I felt had the fewest crevasses. The glacier seemed to be in good condition, but I was wary of possible snow bridges, and so I moved very carefully, probing with my ice axe every few steps, feeling for any hollowness beneath the ice. We wound our way around some of the more obvious crevasses, making sure that we left plenty of space at the ends, between us and the deep icy cracks. My adrenalin was pumping, as it always does when I am leading a climb through such a frightening obstacle course. I was also happy, and enjoying being up so high on the earth in this dazzling white world of ice. It was good *breathing pure air.*

"How's everyone doing?" I yelled back at my climbing partners. "Everyone feeling good?"

Each responded positively, so we continued to move on.

The clouds began drifting in around us, and it started to get dark. There were a few snowflakes beginning to come down now. This wasn't exactly the best place to be in during a storm. I guessed that we were now around the seventeen thousand foot level, and probably had another eight hundred feet of elevation gain to go. I wasn't too worried, since we seemed to have passed most of the crevasses at this point, and as long as the storm didn't get too bad we would just keep heading up the same direction until we came to the crater rim. There is a summit hut sitting right at the highest point, and in an emergency, which it was built for, we could get inside and wait out a storm.

The weather continued to deteriorate, and it was difficult to see ahead of us. My goggles were icing up, and I finally just took them off so that I could see. I shouted back, "We should be getting close to the crater rim. Let's keep moving as fast as we can, and hopefully get to the hut before it gets real bad."

I was sure that they all heard me, but no one answered back, so I just kept moving, trying to pick up the pace a little. *How far is that crater rim? Where is the hut?* I was hoping that we were getting close by now. The snow was coming down heavier now, and my clothes were getting wet from the flakes melting as they clung to my body. It's at times like this that you wonder if you should really be up here. Here we are, over seventeen thousand feet, on a strange mountain in a foreign country. We had very little bivy gear with us, since I knew that this hut existed and had felt that we could rely on it if needed. Our only choice was to keep moving up in the same direction.

Suddenly, in front of me I seemed to see some type of object. *Was this a rock that I was seeing?* My climbing sense told me that it probably wasn't a rock in this area. As I moved closer towards it, I began making out what seemed to be the round metal walls of the hut. I was elated! "Hey you guys! There it is directly ahead of us, the hut!"

I heard response from them this time. "Is that the summit?" asked Bill.

"You'd better believe it!" I shouted back. "Let's get up and inside it, out of this stinking weather!"

The door seemed to be jammed, but with brute force we were finally able to open it. We were soon all inside, and looking around at this mess of a hut. This emergency hut was made out of corrugated metal, anchored down by steel cables, and with a rock base. The floor was supposed to be wood, but it had been torn up ages ago and probably used for firewood, or other basic necessities. Without the wood, the floor was dirt. Little remained of the Plexiglas windows, so basically the windows were wide open. The hut was approximately ten feet in diameter, and eight feet high, large enough for what it had been intended for. Of course both the outside and inside were covered with all sorts of graffiti.

"This isn't exactly the Hilton, but I guess that it'll have to do," joked Steve.

We all chose a place to sit down, trying to keep away from the cold air streaming through the windows. Rather than sit on the cold dirt, I pulled out my sit pad, and plopped down on it. I sat my pack next to me, and leaned back against the cold metal. At least we were out of the storm. We could survive in here. The first time that I saw the hut two years earlier, I was totally turned off by such an ugly structure being put on top of a mountain. I now felt grateful that someone had taken the initiative to haul the materials all the way up here and build it. I just hoped that we would only be spending a few hours here, and not days.

We were pretty quiet at this time, just trying to warm up, and be as comfortable as possible. As my body began getting warmer, my eyes became heavier, and I could barely keep awake. Listening to the wind rattle the hut even made it cozier. I'm sure that the thin air that we were breathing added to our drowsiness, and I felt that I was in a stupor. I was almost asleep when Bill Brownlee, who was right next to me mumbled something.

"What did you say Bill?" I weakly asked.

Bill mumbled again. This time I could make out the comment about something buzzing. He wanted to know if we could hear the buzzing noise?

178

"I don't hear anything bill. Are you sure you hear something?" I asked.

Before he could answer there was a loud explosion! It was ear shattering! It was as if someone had thrown a hand grenade inside the hut! Sparks were flying everywhere and the hut was lit up. Even more frightening were these huge fuzzy red fire balls, the size of basketballs, rolling down the sides of the wall from the top of the hut. We all reacted as if we had bees in our pants, jumping around, trying to avoid these balls. I had heard of "St. Elmo's Fire before; large red fiery balls rolling down mountains during lightning storms, but this was the first time to actually experience them. They only lasted a few seconds, and no one seemed injured from them. Our ears were ringing from the concussion of the explosion, and our hearts were racing.

"That's a lightning strike!" someone yelled. "Let's get out of here now!"

Finally realizing that it was a lightning strike, I yelled back, "Stay where you are! If we go outside we will be totally exposed and will die for sure. For some reason we survived inside, so let's stay here!" I was hoping that I was making the right call.

We just stood there staring at one another. It was hard to believe that we had survived a lightning strike, inside a metal hut, at eighteen thousand feet. I thought I could hear my heart beating it was pounding so hard. We waited, half preparing for another lightning strike. The seconds went by, then the minutes. The wind had died down now, and we could hear the thunder in the clouds above us. It seemed to be moving away from us. Exhausted, we sat down again, waiting and listening, and hoping that another thundercloud wasn't on its way in. More minutes passed by.

Probably half an hour passed by, and the fading thunder slowly left our area. There was actually some sunshine, as the clouds were beginning to thin out, showing blue sky. We anxiously opened the door and looked out. It was actually clearing outside!

We each gingerly stepped out of the hut, looking around, still amazed by what had happened. The sun felt so good, slowly warming our bodies. The air was fresh and clean, and we had one beautiful view of the crater off to our right.

Nervously laughing, we walked around looking over our survival hut from the outside. It certainly didn't seem to be grounded. It was just one enormous lightning rod, located on the summit, sitting higher than any portion of the mountain. How did we survive such a power of nature, and with no injuries?

We decided not to linger around very long, concerned that another storm might be moving in. We began our descent, moving down quickly along the crater, taking us to the Las Cruces, or standard route down the mountain. Soon we were heading down the steep snow, which had softened with the sunshine, allowing us to make good time. As we descended, my mind kept going back to the hut and the terrifying experience. I knew the only way that we could have survived was by a miracle of God. ***God had answered my prayers again!***

****

That evening, after getting cleaned up, and eating a good warm meal, we sat around recalling the events of the day. The rum bottles were opened, and while sipping on our Barcardi, we enjoyed the camaraderie that climbers often do.

Steve was joking as usual, and said something about the **"wienie roast"** that we almost had on the summit. Everyone laughed.

I thought about it a moment, and then just couldn't hold back my tongue at that point. "You know why we almost bought it up there guys?"

"No, why is that Metternich?" they responded.

Half jokingly I asked, "Do you remember on the Rainier climb, and during the lightning storm, the promise that Steve made?"

I didn't have to say any more. Everyone remembered, especially Steve. Suddenly, it became very quiet and serious expressions came on the faces of my friends.

Steve answered, "Yeah! I remember! I blew it!" *And he had.......*

CHAPTER VII

ASSAULT ON THE CASTLE

I have been asked over the years, "What was your most difficult climb?" I have always been reluctant to answer this question. It is very hard to pin point a specific climb as the most difficult since it would require having to take into consideration all the tangibles as well as the intangibles of such an experience. First, I would have to look at the objective dangers faced in a climb; steepness, quality of ice or rock, condition of glaciers and hidden crevasses, avalanche concerns and even altitude. Then, to this list I must add in such factors as weather conditions, time of the year, availability of route descriptions, climbing equipment, and of course climbing partners.

There is one mountain climb that stands out, due to its overall effect it had on me, both physically and mentally. Most climbers, unless living in the Pacific Northwest are not familiar with Mount Adams. It sits in south central Washington State. Even though it is the second highest mountain in the state next to Mount Rainier, with a height of 12,276 feet, it is not generally considered a difficult mountain to climb due to the easiness of the two standard routes. In the summer, these routes are basically long hikes requiring crampons and ice axes, taking from one to two days to complete. A small trail even exists on the southwestern side leading to the summit where at one time there was mining, and donkeys were used to haul supplies up, and then minerals down the mountain. This trail is only visible in late summer and early fall, the rest of the year being covered with snow and ice. Near the summit one can still see the remains of a forest lookout shack used in spotting fires many years ago. Hiking the standard route does not qualify as the ultimate experience in mountaineering even though it requires a lot of motivation and stamina to reach the summit.

Most major mountains, once you are off the standard routes, can offer challenges that will push even the best of climbers. Mount Adams is no exception, having glaciers, steep rock buttresses, and ridges with routes that offer greater challenges. Some sections of the mountain are nearly impossible to climb due to the sheer steepness, rotten rock, and poor ice conditions. Over the years, many climbers have sustained major injuries, and even some deaths have resulted from attempting these little known routes.

In the early months of 1982, my climbing friend, Bob True told me about a book he was reading called "Tales of a Western Mountaineer." It is a biography of a man named C.E. Rusk, an early pioneer who helped settle the southern part of the state of Washington around the Mount Adams area. He was an early explorer of this area, and held a great admiration for the glaciated giant of a mountain. During his explorations of Mt. Adams he became fascinated by a long ridge on the southeast side of the mountain that rose steeply up to a large rock buttress at 11,500 ft. that looked like a castle, and seemed to block the way to the summit. Over many years he attempted to climb this route, a route considered by many as impossible in those days. Finally, after several attempts, he succeeded in climbing it in 1921. He was so enamored with this route that when he died many years later, and based on his last wishes, his son climbed the route, taking his father's cremated ashes in a metal canister, and secured them in the rocks on top of the rock buttress known as the *Castle.*

My friend Bob thought it would be a great idea to attempt this route, and shared this with a group of us. While having coffee and dessert at a local coffee shop, he went over the information he had, especially spending time covering the historical background.

Bob continued, "I don't know what you guys think, but I like the idea of doing a climbing route that few climbers have ever done. I would like to see if Rusk's ashes are still hidden up there in the rocks on the Castle. Anyone else have some thoughts?"

I had brought along Beckey's Cascade Alpine Guide so I interjected, "I have read the route description carefully, what there is of it, and it seems to be doable. Fred Beckey rates it fairly high in difficulty, but not as severe as some of his other climbs. Of course, you can't trust entirely what he has to say about a route because he is a climbing legend. Some of his described routes that I have done in the past were much more difficult to me than the rating he gave it. Even though, I would love to try this route. It would be something new and different. How can you not be excited about a route with features as **Battlement Ridge and the Castle**? It sounds like an assault in the days of the Knights."

The others, Pete Bond, Lando Freisen, and Chip Patton asked to look over the route description in the book. After each had taken his turn reading the description, it was agreed that it would be a **classic climb**, but since the route description seemed to leave out a lot of detail, there were reservations about climbing it.

Bob came up with an idea. "I have a friend who is a member of a flying club, and possibly we could rent their airplane for a day and I could talk my friend into flying a few of us to Mt. Adams to get a look at the climb."

"How many seats in the airplane?" Pete asked.

"I believe it is a four seater," Bob replied.

Maybe our minds were not functioning properly, thinking only of the challenge ahead, as we barely questioned the wisdom of having a novice pilot fly us in a small aircraft in order to get a close view of the mountain. How capable was this guy as a pilot, anyway? After discussing our concerns, Bob said he would check with his friend, finding out the availability of the airplane, the date, and also, how many hours of experience he had in piloting a small aircraft in the Northwest? If everything worked out, and the pilot seemed capable, it was decided that Bob, Pete and myself would be the ones going. The other two potential members of our team would wait and see what we came up with.

The next day, after Bob had checked on the pilot and the airplane, he calls and tells me that the only date the airplane, a small Cessna, was available was on Friday, the day before our scheduled drive to the mountain. It didn't seem like a prudent plan since we would be gone most of Friday, probably getting back late that night, and then driving up the next day, a five hour drive to the trailhead. This would be followed by a hike of four or five miles to base camp. Even though it would add to our tiring trip, Bob and I felt it was necessary in order to determine whether this was a worthy objective or just a *crazy idea!*

I replied to Bob," I'm willing if you are. How about our pilot, do you trust him?"

"He just got his solo license, but seems to be an intelligent and conservative type guy. He is a member of the flight club that leases the airplane. I doubt that they would trust it to him if he wasn't capable."

"Oh great!" I responded. "I'm holding you responsible. If we crash and die, my family will kill you!"

"Hell of a deal!" came his reply.

Very early on July 16, 1982, the three of us, plus the pilot met at the small Salem, Oregon airport. After introducing ourselves to the pilot, we gulped down our coffee that we had just bought at the little cafe at the airport. Could this possibly be our *last meal?* We grunted as we squeezed into the cramped seating of the small four seat aircraft, especially Bob with his six foot five frame. We each brought along a small pack. Mine contained a camera with a tele-photo lense, a set of binoculars, map, climbing guide, water and a couple of granola bars. Once our seat belts were fastened, the pilot turned on the engine, and soon the single-blade propeller was whirling. Taxiing to the end of the runway we waited for the approval of the tower. It took only moments, and then our pilot opened the throttle until the plane was shaking, and then letting go of the brakes we quickly raced down the runway and lifted into the sky.

The weather in Oregon and southern Washington was clear; a beautiful day with relatively very little wind. The airplane lazily cruised north, heading directly towards Mt. St. Helens, which could be seen off in the distance with its easily recognizable cone, now with a large amount of it blown off by the 1980 volcanic eruption. As the plane moved smoothly in the air, I examined the landscape below; the beautiful northwest, with its abundance of forests, rivers and lakes. From our altitude there was a carpet of green for as far as the eye could see divided only by snaking rivers, large lakes, and a few ridges.

Within the hour, we were closing in on Mt. St. Helens. Banking to the right, we turned east heading towards Mt. Adams, a huge mound-shaped mountain glistening off in the distance.

We flew in from the west, and as we approached the large mountain, the pilot angled towards the southern flank of the mountain, so as not to approach too close, and then headed directly east again. Off in the distance you could see our objective; the long ridge named Battlement, and high on the ridge, almost at our same attitude the enormous rock buttress called the Castle.

We closed in slowly towards the mountain, trying to maintain a mile or so of distance so as not to get sucked into the mountain by a sudden down draft that mountains are notorious for. As we drew closer, I could see that the steep ridge seemed to nearly level out, just on left of the Castle. The only way over to the Castle from there was a very steep snow traverse running east above the bergschrund (a huge crevasse where the glacier ends and separates from the rock and dirt). Just above the crevasse, and running parallel beneath our traverse was a large ice cliff. We would be a hundred feet above the huge cliff, on steep ice. Indeed, it looked *scary!*

If we succeeded up the ridge, and were next able to traverse the steep ice, the greatest challenge still lay ahead, the Castle itself. The guidebook mentions climbing a gully-chimney on breccia, or rotten rock, that takes you two hundred feet up to the crest of the Castle. Using my binoculars, I strained to find the gully-chimney described. It looked like there was more than one gully, but which one was the correct one, and would it lead all the way up? I could see that the only way to the top of the castle would be up one of these slots. We couldn't go around either ends of the Castle, because they were blocked by icefalls. The icefall on the left of the Castle seemed to go partially up the side of the Castle, swing around behind, and then drop straight off. The icefall on the right was a spectacular vertical cliff of over two hundred feet, the top of which was almost adjacent to the top of the Castle.

"Can we circle back and make another run at it? Maybe a little closer this time," I asked.

"Sure, we have plenty of fuel and lots of time left. I'll try to get in a little closer, but not too close because of possible down drafts," the pilot shouted back.

As we made our approach, much closer this time, we were immediately buffeted by the wind. Suddenly our little airplane was jumping up and down and sideways. It was nerve wracking to be tossed about in that small airplane. I tried to focus my binoculars on the route but was unable to keep them steady. I then grabbed my camera for some more pictures. Within a few minutes we were out of range again, managing a couple of pictures, and then we headed away from the mountain.

I'm not sure what we had accomplished. Because of what I saw, I did not have positive feelings about accomplishing the climb. It certainly would be a challenge. The ridge was scary, steep, dropping off on both sides, and probably composed of rotten rock and sand. The snow traverse looked very steep, taking you up to the base of a 200 ft. rock buttress, which was probably rotten to the core. We hadn't even talked about the other side of the Castle.

Once on top of the Castle, what would it be like getting off the other side?

On our flight back to Salem we landed at the Hillsdale Airport to refuel, where we enjoyed a sandwich and beer in the airport lounge and discussed the options. After downing a couple of quick beers, we tried to decide on whether to head up the next day and attempt the route. Since time and money was already invested in this trip, we all voted to "go for it." We knew that the climb would be demanding and very time consuming and we would not be coming down the same route as going up. Therefore, an early start on summit day was imperative, especially if we hoped to get back to base camp the same night. But, just in case, we agreed that each person must carry some bivouac gear in case we had to spend the night high up the mountain.

I lay in bed that night thinking about the exciting day that we just had. The flight up and back, and viewing the spectacular mountain and the route from the air was in itself a wonderful experience. I thought about the mountain. It was much larger than I had imagined, having many large glaciers flowing down its sides with cascading icefalls, and steep cliffs. I could feel my heart race as I thought of the challenge ahead. Climbing a mountain and a route for the first time, with little available route description would truly be an alpine experience. Finally, I dozed off.

****

The alarm startled me. It was already 3:45 a.m. and I felt like I had just gone to sleep. Boy, this was going to be a long day. I jumped up, dressed, and had a quick bowl of cereal. I gulped a cup of coffee as I finished putting the last items into my pack. I was feeling a little rummy after having only a few hours of sleep, and I hoped that I wouldn't leave anything important behind.

I could see the other climbers sorting gear as I drove up to the parking lot where we would leave most of the cars. "Good morning guys. Is everyone ready for a new adventure in mountaineering?"

"Sure Metternich! We're ready to **rock and roll**," answered one of our group.

"I don't know why I participate in a sport that requires you to get up in the middle of the night," bemoans Pete.

Bob responds, "Because someone's got to do it!"

"I could be home curled up to a warm body," adds Lando.

"But you would miss out on all this fun" says Pete, followed by a chuckle.

We all laugh...

As we finish sorting our gear, I realize that I must carry many types of protection devices since we will be climbing across crevassed glaciers, up rotten ridges and rock climbing. *I need to be organized. It would be embarrassing if I left anything important behind.*

Soon we were on our way, all five of us riding in Pete's VW Vanagan. We drove north to Portland, Oregon, and then took the Columbia River Highway east. Near Hood River we crossed over the Columbia River into White Salmon, Washington. From there we drove north along the White Salmon River until we turned off and headed up the forest service roads which took us to the trail head for the standard southwest route and other westerly routes located at the 6,500 ft. level. We would only be following this trail a short distance, and then we would head easterly cross country, passing just below the Mazama Glacier, to a camp area located between the Mazama Glacier and the Klickitat Glacier. We would not see the Klickitat Glacier until we were on the small ridge next to it, where our camp would be located.

The cross-country hiking was strenuous as we had to cross over large rocks, and work our way around and through brush and small trees most of the way. After crossing over a couple of small ridges we were finally able to get onto the snowfield that made our hiking much easier. We now moved quickly, and in a few hours we had reached our base camp.

As soon as we had picked out our tent sites, I dropped my pack, and began hiking up the small ridge next to our camp. It felt good to have the heavy pack off my shoulders, and with this weight taken off, my legs felt like coiled springs. I almost felt like I could bounce up to the top of the ridge. As I approached the top, I suddenly caught the view of the entire Klickitat Glacier, running from the ice fall next to the Castle, down the steep slopes, then forming the huge flowing river of ice, sliced up with crevasses, lower and lower until it passed just below me. Looking directly across, I could see that the portion of the Glacier we would be crossing was a jumbled mess of small crevasses, strewn with dirt and rock fall. It looked to be around a half mile across to Battlement Ridge.

I felt the adrenaline beginning to flow in me as I searched out our prospective route across the glacier, and the area where we would gain the ridge. I needed to memorize as much of the terrain as possible, because at a very early start, it would still be dark, making it much more difficult. Getting off track in the darkness can cost a group important time, making a difference on whether you get back to base camp that night, or spend a cold night bivvied on the side of the mountain. It always makes me a little nervous when I think that my mistakes can affect the whole group relying on me. I guess that is the main reason most climbers don't want to lead climbs, but would rather follow someone else and just let their minds relax.

I had seen enough. The route had everything to offer in climbing, and it would offer each of us a rugged challenge. I glanced once more at the Castle high above me. It seemed to stare down at me ominously, saying, "*I dare you to come up here!*" I headed back down to my tent site.

****

It was still dark as the five of us headed out at a little after 4:00 a.m. the next morning. The packs seemed heavy; they always do, even though we left tents, cooking gear, sleeping bags and other extra gear at camp. We moved quickly, plunging and sliding down the steep scree on the ridge to the glacier just below. I had decided we would head across the glacier without roping up, hoping that the ropes would not be necessary, thus saving us time. The crevasses were small, and the footing good, and the ice mixed with dirt gave us good traction. The beam from my headlamp lit up the ice far ahead of me, allowing me good visual perception to find a route through and around the crevasse field. I was amazed at how easy it was winding our way over the glacier. I was glad that I had decided not to use the ropes for safety, even though it would have been the prudent thing to do, as we made so much better time without them.

Within a half an hour we were at the other side of the glacier. We stopped, pulled out our water bottles for some liquid, and tried to regain our breaths.

"Now the fun really begins!" I was referring to the steep flank of the ridge that we needed to climb up, composed of soft, loose scree, in order to gain the top of the ridge.

As I headed up, after every few steps I would slide back a step due to the soft, unstable dirt and rock beneath my feet. Each time this occurred, I lost my rhythm, and had to gasp for air. Take a step; then another; then another; then slide backwards. I leaned over, hyper-ventilated, then moved on.

Finally gaining the ridge top, I turned around and shouted back, "Looks like a good spot to take a break. Let's make it no more than fifteen here."

I took off my pack, dropped it to the ground and then sat down on it. Pulling out my water bottle and some gorp, I watched as my team came puffing up the last few feet.

"**Sheeiite!**" yelled Bob; one of his favorite expletives. After pausing to catch his breath, he continued," Gary, what does the ridge look like?"

A glow was beginning in the eastern sky, and the ridge was beginning to lighten up enabling us to see some distance up our route.

"I really can't tell yet Bob, but it doesn't look too bad. Not too steep either. You can see there will be some large rocks in our way that we will have to navigate around, but the ridge looks wide enough to do it. The footing is a lot better here than what we just came up."

"I hope so. That scree really takes the energy out of you!"

We took our rest of fifteen minutes or more, enjoying the scenery, all the while replenishing ourselves with water and various snacks. Not much was said, but I was sure that many questioning thoughts were going through my fellow climber's minds.

After our break, we were up and on our way again, heading up the long ridge. The ridge was not too steep, and was bare of snow except for a few small patches in shady areas around rocks. We moved at a good pace. As we came to the large rocks, we were able to maneuver around them, sometimes to the right, and sometimes around the left. As it became lighter, we could look down both flanks of the ridge and view the glaciers. The Castle was clearly visible high above us, yet as we moved higher and higher, it didn't seem to be getting any closer, only larger. I tried to look ahead and see the upper part of the ridge, but it was always blocked from view by the rocks ahead. I wondered: *Will the going be this easy the rest of the way?*

I felt good, and didn't seem to be forcing myself up this ridge. It was still hard work; climbing is always hard work. The other guys on this climb with me were in excellent condition, and easily kept up with me as we moved quickly up. What a beautiful day! Even though there was the possibility that we could be forced back at some point in the climb, it was still worth it, just being on this beautiful mountain at this moment in time.

After working our way around the last of the large rocks, we came to a section where the ridge began narrowing. We were now at over 9,000 ft. in altitude. The ridge was not only narrowing but was becoming more sandy, and the footing less stable. A couple of hundred feet later, the ridge began leveling and quickly narrowed. I looked ahead of me on the ridge and couldn't believe what I saw! Just before the ridge angled to the right it narrowed down to a width of only a few feet, with drop-offs on both sides of it. As I came closer, I could see that the only way we could continue up the ridge was to cross the narrow section that extended thirty to forty feet in length.

Holy cow! How to get across this section? This wasn't even in the route description by Beckey. I had never seen anything like it. I had been across narrow snow bridges in the past, but this was dirt, and had a top layer of sand mixed with rock; highly unstable and looking as if sections of it could slide off at any moment. Adding to this, it dropped off on the left side almost straight down a thousand feet to the Klickitat icefall. On the right side, even though not a vertical drop, it was steep, having large loose rocks protruding through the sand and soil, and it fell an equal distance to a snowfield, and then to the Rusk Glacier.

I thought to myself, *If, we can't get across this section, then our climb is finished. We won't even get to the Castle*!

I certainly didn't want to turn around, and I was sure the others didn't either, but this section looked frightening. Could I shimmy across this section? I knew that I certainly wasn't going to attempt walking across it.

As the guys came up behind me, Bob asked, "What the heck do we have here?"

"It doesn't look good," I answered. "If we don't get across this section, then we head home," I said with a worried tone in my voice. Looking at the narrow trail of sand and rock for a moment, I continued, "Somehow, I am going to get across this section even if I have to crawl." Then I turned to Pete who was carrying the rope, "Pete, put me on belay. Bob, be a back-up to Pete."

"Got you matey!" answered Pete.

As the climbing rope was being uncoiled, I took one end, tying a figure eight knot, and then clipped the rope, using a carabiner, onto my harness. Pete proceeded to uncoil the rope until there was enough to allow me to get across the narrow section. After Pete got himself into belay position, and with Bob backing him, he asked, "On belay?"

I responded, "Belay on."

"Climbing!" I said as I moved cautiously forward and approached the beginning of the narrow bridge. I slowly placed each step, testing the stableness, concerned that the sand and rocks could slide off at any moment, throwing me down the steep side. I eased my feet a couple of more steps then decided that I wouldn't go any further standing up. The only way across this section was to sit down and scoot across. I sat down, letting my legs hang over the west side of the ridge, directly above the Klickitat Glacier below.

194

The sun was now up high in the sky and I could feel the heat on my back. I began to sweat, and the perspiration started running down my forehead into my eyes, stinging them. I placed my hands below me, pushing my body along the bridge sideways, inch-by-inch. Every few moments a large amount of sand would slide from underneath me down off the ridge, triggering small rock, then larger rocks, followed by great amounts of rocks crashing onto the ice-fall far below. This sent large clouds of dust into the air, followed by a thundering roar as the debris raced down the icefall, and then the sound would fade away. Each time this happened, my heart raced.

I yelled back jokingly, "I sure hope that there is some rock left for you guys to come across on!" My biggest concern was that I could slide off at any moment, and even if Pete could hold me, I would bang into the rock and scree, and be left hanging down over the side, with no way to get back up, except to be physically pulled up. I thought to myself, ***get it out of your mind!***

Carefully, I worked my way across the remaining expanse. As I reached the wider part of the ridge, I carefully got up onto my feet. "That wasn't all that bad," I yelled back.

"Oh Sure," Bob joked, "Do you want to come back and show us again how it's done? I didn't take it all in."

"I would love to, but I don't want to keep you from enjoying it," I answered back. I added, I think that we should attach another rope on the next person and throw the end to me so that they will be belayed on both ends. After doing so, I then waited nervously as each one came carefully across, sending more avalanches of sand and rock down onto the Klickitat.

Once everyone was across, I commented "It looks alright ahead. I don't see any more of this, thank God!" Let's move ahead a ways and take another break."

Once again, after a short break we were on our way. I was anxious to get up the final stages of the ridge and be able to see how assessable the steep area below the Castle would be. The climbing was easy, but I still did not like the consistency of the scree and sand that we were on. Just ahead there seemed to be one last small bulge that we would need to cross over, and then we would be close to the saddle that lay between us and the steep flanks of the Castle.

Because of the exposure on the left, we were forced to traverse around the right of the bulge. The right side slanted steeply and we were looking directly down at the Rusk Glacier below. Even though it wasn't too steep, the footing was terribly loose and slow going, and we had to search for small rocks to step on to prevent sliding. Our movement was slow and it was eating up much valuable time. I had an idea. I would try to sort of jog, hoping that my momentum would keep me from sliding. It worked, and soon I had covered the nearly two hundred feet to the saddle where I stopped. This was a good place to rest and take our next break. The others imitated me and were soon gathered around for our break.

It was an impressive spot for a break. Looking up and to our right loomed the huge rock buttress known as the Castle. Directly to our right was the steep traverse that we would soon be on. It was probably sixty degrees in steepness. Just below the traverse was the ice cliff, then under it, the bergschrund, or crevasse. Even though we couldn't see the crevasse from our angle, we all knew exactly where it lay. Looking over the terrain, I decided that I would traverse diagonally upwards towards the Castle, thus distancing ourselves from the ice cliff and the crevasse below.

"Let's uncoil the two ropes and clip into our harnesses. We'll start out with our crampons, and also wear helmets from here on."

"Can you see our gully, the way up through the Castle from here?" Pete asked.

"Not yet, but I am hoping it will come into view as we get closer."

As soon as everyone was ready, out came the ice axes, and we moved out; three people on my rope, and two on the second. The sun was really beating down on our backs now, making it quite warm. The snow was softening, and it was sun-cupped, which are big hollows in the snow made by constant melting and re-freezing. Being able to step into these sun made steps made for easy and safe placement of crampons.

I angled up the very steep snow, ever mindful of what was below me. Soon, the sweat was pouring down into my eyes, and I had to stop, take off my helmet, wrap a handkerchief around my forehead, and then put my helmet back on. Even though it was hot, I felt good, and the adrenaline flowing through me gave me the energy to move quickly. Even though I was moving quickly, I did so carefully, making sure that each placement of my feet and ice-axe were done exact. ***No falling here I told myself!***

The air was thin, as we were now over ten thousand feet, but we continued to move quickly upward. Within an hour we had climbed nearly a thousand feet and were a hundred feet below the Castle. I could now see the various cracks and gullies, but which one do we take? I remembered the picture in the guidebook showing a slot near the far right of the Castle and headed in that direction. As we came nearer, I could see a cave like opening. I headed towards that opening near the corner of the Castle.

As I approached the opening, I could see that it was large and dark inside, almost void of snow except for a few patches on the floor of the cave. There was a small ledge of dirt in front of me just above the last few feet of snow we were on, and I worked my way up to it. I stepped onto the red dirt. I then moved up to the opening, peering inside, hoping that I would see some way up through the rock. There was a narrow rounded wall directly in front of me, leading up to what looked like a ledge. ***This may be the way up***, I thought. The rock was steep, but looked climbable if it wasn't too rotten. There were small knobs protruding out of the breccia, possibly secure enough to grasp with your fingers, or to place the front points of the crampons on.

Before entering the cave, I turned my attention to the outside corner of the Castle that was just a few yards away. "Give me some slack, I want to look around this corner," I shouted to my rope mates. "Possibly an easier way up." As they moved up, giving me slack in the rope, I moved towards the corner. When I came to the corner and peered around it, my breath was taken away by what I saw. The Castle dropped off a couple of hundred feet directly below me to an ice flow. This ice flow ran from the top of the Castle, down it flanks, separating the Castle from the ice cliffs directly across from me. The ice flow was almost vertical and made up of hard blue ice. The vertical ice cliffs adjoining it were enormous, around two hundred feet in height. They stood there, also icy blue in color, now glistening with the sunshine on them.

So much for that! We would have to try the ramp in the cave.

"Okay, let's head back to that cave. That's got to be the way up."

I walked back along the path above the snow, and was soon inside the cave. I shouted back at Pete, "I'm going to try this wall with my crampons, and see how far I get. Let's keep roped up even though it probably won't do any good in a fall." I noticed that my voice echoed off the walls of the cave, adding to the eeriness.

As I placed my foot on the breccia, and made my first move up, I realized that it wasn't rock but clay, and that the protruding rocks were not secure. My crampons helped, biting into the clay and giving me some support. I placed my hands on the little rocks above me, trying not to put any weight on them, but just using them for balance. I used the pick of the ice ax when needing more support, by driving the sharp point into the soft clay. Slowly, I moved up.

Bob, who was on the other end of the rope called up to me, "What's it like, Gary?"

"It's really rotten, Bob," I shouted down nervously. "Just be darn careful because if you fall, you will pull me off for sure," I added.

As I moved up, once in a while I dislodged small rocks, and they would shower those below me. When I had climbed up about fifty feet I saw a ramp that led off the rock wall that I was on. The ramp was narrow, possibly eighteen inches wide and it angled up to my left. The lighting was poor and I couldn't see exactly how far the ramp led. I moved up. Occasionally, I could feel tautness in the rope, and knew that Pete, who was on the center of the rope, was struggling to climb up below me.

I was now at the ramp and just about to take a step onto it when I heard a roaring sound and felt the vibration that almost knocked me off my stance. It was the deafening sound of a huge chunk of ice breaking off the ice cliffs and crashing down the gully next to the Castle. It was followed by tons of ice and rock sweeping down the mountain onto the glacier below. It only lasted a few terrifying seconds. Soon, spindrift and dust from the avalanche floated up and into our cave.

For a while I didn't hear anyone below me. "Is everyone alright?" I shouted.

Then I heard some cussing, followed by Bob shouting back, "Yep, but the son of a **B** nearly scared you know what out of me!"

I waited a moment until my body quit trembling, then began moving up the ramp again. That was **unnerving**, I thought. **What's next**?

Now and then I would get a strong tug on the rope below me. It was probably Pete losing a handhold, or his feet slipping. **Please don't pull me off this!** I thought.

I could see a small amount of light up ahead. It seemed to be shining through a small opening and looked to be forty or more feet away. **Maybe that's the way up to the top of the Castle.**

Suddenly, I came to the end of the ramp. It looked like it had broken off, and now there was a void between the rest of the ramp on the other side, a couple of yards ahead, and me. To my right was a blank wall. I noticed that where the ramp had broken away, there was a small lip remaining of a couple inches wide running along the wall towards the other part of the ramp. I looked around me. No other way to go. **I don't think going down is an option either.** If I could just use my ice axe, and get the pick into the soft wall, it might support me enough to use my crampons and toe across this expanse.

"Hey guys, stay where you are, and prepare yourself for a fall. I have to move across a bad spot. I may be falling!"

From down below, "Be careful!"

It's amazing how much your climbing partners trust you, especially after climbing together for many years. Since they couldn't see me, they probably didn't realize the precarious situation that I was in. If I fell now, there would be no way to hold me, and my fall would yank them right off the rock also. It would be nasty, if not fatal.

I grabbed the adze, the larger portion of the ice axe, opposite the pick, and stabbed the small sharp pick into the wall.

The wall was soft, possibly from the dampness inside. The pick was in and it didn't break out. Next, I faced the wall, and kicked the two points of the crampons on my right foot into the clay above the small lip. They held. I carefully swung my left leg around and did the same. Slowly, I pulled the ice-axe pick out, moved it to my left, and then forced it into the wall again. I alternated doing this for the next couple of yards, until I reached the other end of the ramp. I had made it to the other side.

"**Holy Moly, I'm across!** I yelled down, "I'll find a good position to belay, and then I'll bring you guys up." At least, they will have a good belay from me.

I moved up the ramp until I found a secure spot to belay from, and then I had the others on my rope move up.

As my partners made it to where I was, "Welcome to I don't know where," I joked. "You see that light up there? I am hoping that's the way to the top." I thought to myself, *if it's not, we're screwed, because we'd be at a dead end!* "Let's un-rope here, making it easier to pass these rocks in our way. Bob, coil the rope, and then you guys wait here for me, and I will go check it out."

"You've got it! Boy, do I hope that's the way," Bob answered.

I climbed around and then over some boulders blocking my path towards the light. *This has to be it!* I thought. I felt an excitement as I moved forward. I came up beneath a small hole, possibly eight to ten feet up above me. I could see sunshine and blue sky outside the hole. *Now to get up to the hole!* There was one boulder in my way, extending about half way up to the hole. I climbed onto it, and shimmied up to the hole.

Looking at the exit hole, I knew that my body and the pack

would not fit through at the same time. I took off my pack and dropped it below me. I yelled down, "I'm going up through the hole. Would you bring my pack up?"

I put my arms through the hole above me, found something to hold onto, and squeezed myself up through.

Immediately, I felt the warm sunshine on my face. As I glanced around, **this is it! This is the top of the Castle.** I peered at the strange looking landscape. It was very flat, and made up of dark, volcanic looking rock, strewn with small pebbles. In my mind I imagined the landscape on the moon looking like this. In a strange way it was very beautiful to me.

Now, I needed to get my buddies up. I moved back to the hole, and putting my head down through the opening, shouted for them to come on up.

Soon, Pete was handing me my pack, and then his. He grunted his way up through the tight hole. "Wow! This is it!"

A few minutes later Bob was pulling himself through. A half an hour later the other two climbers made their way up to the top.

All five of us sat there together, and even though tired we were exhilarated knowing that we had succeeded in doing what we had set out to do. A cool, crisp breeze was blowing, and the warm sunshine felt good as we sat on the pebbled surface, eating our late lunch and celebrating.

"That was some kind of rock climb," commented Lando. "And that final move up through the hole was really something special," he added.

"I'm glad that none of you are fat guys. We would have had to leave you behind!" I said jokingly.

****

We had almost forgot to look for C.E. Rusk's canister and his cremated remains. We all began searching around the rocks near the edge of the Castle. Soon, the canister was located, along with the metal plaque with his name on it. I was amazed that the canister still existed after so many years, not having been thrown over the side by some vandal. Maybe, it was due to climbers just not knowing about it, or possibly because of the caliber of climbers doing this route. I took the canister and asked that someone take a picture of me holding it and the plaque on my knee.

A tube-like container was also found nearby, and inside were scraps of paper with names and notations of other climbers successfully climbing this route. There were less than a dozen, with most of the dates going back to the forties and fifties. Some of the names I recognized as famous climbers of a time gone by.

When we had finished our lunch and were re-hydrated with water, we again lifted our stiff bodies off the ground, and put our packs back on. It was now time to get off the Castle and continue our climb. We all had been so excited about our summiting the Castle we had nearly forget that we still had to get off the other side down to the glacier, and then climb another couple of hours to the true summit that was waiting approximately two thousand feet higher. It was nearly four in the afternoon by this time.

"Let's go over to the other side and take a look. The guide book doesn't say much about it, so let's hope there is an easy way down." I was confident that it wouldn't be overly difficult.

We hiked directly across the flat surface to the other side and looked for a way down. It was over a hundred feet down to the glacier. The way down was obvious; a steep, dirt slope, littered with small rocks. A rappel would be the way to go, so I searched for a solid rock on which to anchor the rope.

None of the rocks were solid. They were all sitting on top of the scree and probably wouldn't hold our weight. Scrambling down without being roped wasn't a good option either, since just left of the scree slope there was an ice chute that curved down to the Klickitat icefall below. If someone slipped into that chute, they would be gone for sure. *I must belay each climber down, one by one.*

I sat down in a sitting belay position, and got my feet as secure as possible. The guys each took their turn clipping the end of the rope into their harnesses, and climbing down the slope. It was loose, and every so often a foot would slip on small rocks, causing the climber to fall on his rear. *How am I going to get down this without a belay?*

Soon it was my turn. I told them to pull the rope down. It was totally useless to me. I had finger-less gloves that I had worn up, so I kept them on just in case I fell, to avoid tearing my flesh on the small sharp rocks. Down I started, being ever so careful not to slip and lose my balance. I thought of sliding down on my rear, but was afraid that I would lose control and veer over to the left into the ice chute.

About half way down I suddenly slipped on loose rock and started sliding quickly down the slope towards the ice chute. I rolled over quickly onto my stomach, extending my arms and legs, with my hands spread out above me. I continued to slide. I could feel pain in my exposed fingers as I slid over small sharp rocks embedded in the dirt. At last I stopped, just a few feet away from the bottom, and the ice chute.

I looked at my fingers. They were shredded, and bleeding. I was dripping red drops onto the pure white snow. *A small price to pay*, I thought to myself.

"Are you okay?" someone asked.

I answered affirmative as I dusted myself off. "Just a little blood. I'll stick my hands in the snow and the bleeding should stop." I didn't want to admit it, but my fingers were stinging badly.

We clipped into the ropes, and soon began winding our way up the glacier. Time and time again I turned around and glanced back at the top of the Castle that was now becoming smaller behind us. What a day! We were heading for the summit.

An hour and a half later we were on the true summit of Mt. Adams. It was after six p.m., and we knew that we wouldn't reach base camp until after dark, since we had to descend the Mazama Glacier, being ever careful of crevasses. I thought of base camp. We would all be exhausted from the eighteen hours of climbing. Then, the 151 rum would come out, we'd have drinks and swap stories, celebrating the day's events. But, this was now. We were on the summit, and the feelings of success were intoxicating to the soul. Tears came into my eyes from the deep sense of joy that I felt. We took turns shaking hands and hugging each other. The cameras came out, and we took many pictures of this special time.

The scenery atop a mountain is majestic, seemingly with the world laid out below you. We soaked it in. The sky was changing color from blue to orange as the sun dropped lower in the western sky. The air was clean and crisp. We were five lonely specks on top of a mountain, *breathing pure air*, and taking in the beauty of God's nature. The world didn't know nor cared that we were here, standing alone above the clouds. We didn't care either whether the world knew. This was our moment, and only ours. The memories of this experience would be with us until the day our last breaths were gone.

****

We all felt that we had achieved a **Classic climb.** The five of us also swore that we would never subject ourselves to such torture again; not this climb; not this route! **Never!** Women go through the pain of childbirth, often swearing that they will never have children again. But, soon they forget the pain that they endured, and eventually desire having another child. Like these women, we would also forget, and four years later I led the same climb again, accompanied by two of the original mental patients: Bob True and Pete Bond. Two others also joined us. This next time though, there would be no celebration, because when it was over, we were just **too exhausted!**

CHAPTER VIII

BITS AND PIECES
(SOME VERY SHORT STORIES)

FOLLOW THAT TRAIL

In the spring of 1977, during the earlier years of my climbing, I decided to climb a route on Mt. Hood that I had never climbed before. I had read about it, and knew that though the route was not an easy one, and it was one of the more popular on the mountain. I could find no one in our climbing club that had done the route before, so I decided to study the guidebook and do it on my own. The route was called Wy'east, a name taken from the Native Americans that had lived near the mountain. I decided to take my wife who was only into her second year of climbing, hence much less experienced than me. It shouldn't be too difficult I thought, as I knew that many climbers do the route each year, and there was a good chance that there would be other climbers on the route, and we could just follow them.

We started up the mountain a little after mid-night from Timberline Lodge. It was very dark that night with no moon at all, and so headlamps had to be used from the very beginning to see our way. When the moon is out, it can be quite lit up on the pure white snow, making it unnecessary to use headlamps. The description in the guide book said to veer to the east from the lodge, and head up alongside the White Water canyon. Later, we would need to drop down into the canyon and cross it, then head straight toward the Steel Cliffs. There was an alternative, and that would be to continue heading straight ahead, staying close to the standard route, and then to cross over the upper part of the snow covered canyon just below the steep Steel Cliffs. The Steel Cliffs are located at approximately 9,500 ft.

Since it was so dark, it was impossible to see where we needed to drop down into the canyon, and cross, and so we continued going straight ahead. Up above us, I could see the light from other climber's headlamps, and decided to follow them. Maybe they would know where to cross.

We moved quickly, and as the sky began getting light from the first rays of the sun, we could see that we were catching up with the other climbers. I also noticed that we were approaching what looked like a crevasse field. Apparently we had gone too far and had passed the cross over point, and now we would need to try the alternative route higher up. *Hopefully those guys know the way through or around the crevasses,* I thought to myself. Yet, the way they were moving and seemingly searching around made me feel that they were also lost.

Since we were moving much faster than them, we quickly caught up. "Good morning guys." They seem startled that we had caught up to them so quickly. "It sure is broken up here. Have you done this route before"? I asked.

They answered back that they hadn't. We chatted for a couple of minutes, then everyone started taking their packs off for a much needed break. The spot seemed like a good one, just a few yards away from the crevasses and on safe snow. As we had been climbing steadily for a few hours, it was nice taking off the packs, sitting down, and enjoying some liquid and energy snacks. Since we had not yet roped, this would be an appropriate place to rope up before entering the crevasse field. As we sat resting, I was hoping that they roped up first, and then we could follow them through the crevasses. Besides, three on their rope was much safer than two of us on a rope.

Fifteen minutes or so went by, and I realized that they were in no hurry to leave before us. They had not even started getting their harnesses on yet. It seemed that we may need to go first. I turned to my wife, and said that I felt we should say a little prayer for our safety and the safety of the others. My wife agreed, and we said a prayer. Anxious to be on our way, and confident that our new friends were going to out wait us, I got up and uncoiled the rope, laying it out to clip into. They seemed content to just watch us, and I noticed that they had not even begun uncoiling their rope. I wondered, *are they going to attempt going through the crevasses without being roped up?*

When we were ready, I headed to the left of the crevasses, looking ahead to see if I could lead us around and above the crevasse field. As I moved forward, the rope stretched out between us, and after about forty feet, it became taut, telling me that we were now in the safest position for a fall. If either climber falls into a crevasse, the rope being stretched between the two creates friction as it slides along the snow. It is possible for one individual to actually hold two or three others that have fallen into a crevasse if the rope is long enough between climbers and stretched out properly. Getting out of the crevasse is another matter though. As I moved ahead, I prayed, *Dear Lord, give me great wisdom in leading everyone through this area.*

We needed to cross over to the right somewhere, but the crevasses were too numerous at this section of the snow field, so I continued along the steep snow bank on my left. The angle became steeper and steeper, and seemed to be leading up to a knoll ahead. I continued on and as I reached the top of the knoll, I was grateful to see that the snow seemed to fan out, leading up and around the crevasses to my right. I had concentrated on the crevasses so much that I failed to notice that the Steel Cliffs were now looming high above us. *This must be where we head across, I thought. We can't go much further.*

I searched ahead following the line of direction that I was heading, and then I thought I saw what looked like a foot trail in the snow a couple of hundred feet further, that ran horizontally across a snow ramp. *Hotdog! These must be the tracks of the previous day's climbers.* I yelled back, "This is our way across." Being excited, I quickly headed towards the seemed to be path.

As I approached, I could see that the trail looked to be sunken a few inches below the level of the snow. *Probably a large group of climbers had come across it, I thought.* It even looked discolored from their boots. *A perfect way across!* I stopped for a couple of seconds, and looking back at my wife, I said that I thought this was the way others had come before us. I also saw the other climbers coming into view a little further back. They were following us, and it made me feel good that I had found the way across the crevasse field. *Where was their rope?*

I felt a rush of adrenaline. Soon we would be across this crevassed area, heading towards the ridge and away from the Steel Cliffs above. Even though there would be other unfamiliar parts of the climb, I was confident they could be overcome just like we had this section. I moved ahead along the path, tugging at my partner behind me. What happened next will be forever embedded in my mind.

I was about one third of the way across the sunken snow path and about to take my next step when the snow suddenly collapsed below me. *I had been on a snow bridge covering a crevasse!* What I had thought was a climber's trail, was actually where the snow bridge had been melting and beginning to droop. *What an idiot I was! I had read about crevasses, and knew that the sinking effect was something to stay away from. It hadn't even occurred to me!*

Like an animal falling through a man-made trap into a pit, I was falling through a large hole into a deep, blue iced

210

crevasse. In mille-seconds, and as I was falling, I was able to see everything around and beneath me. The route that I had taken was directly on the crevasse, following it diagonally. Where I had fallen through, the crevasse was approximately four to five feet wide, and the ice was over a foot thick. Ahead, I saw that the crevasse became wider and wider, and there was nothing but a blue icy void below me. The crevasse had to be sixty to ninety feet deep.

When an animal falls into a trap, it happens so fast that it doesn't have time to respond. But, as I fell, my body instantly swung around to the right with my arms out, and then the palms of my hands came down on the broken off lip of the crevasse. My pack weighed nearly forty pounds, yet my arms incredibly held me up, with my body hanging in the crevasse. I heard the broken off snow as it crashed down below me into the depths of the crevasse. I yelled out to my wife forty feet behind me. "I'm in a crevasse!" My wife had just been standing there watching this whole thing, but then dropped down into the self-arrest position. At that point it would have done me no good at all.

Here I was, hanging in a crevasse with a heavy pack on and with my arms partially extended out in front of me, yet I didn't feel any pressure on my arms. *It was as though something was holding me up from below. It had to be a miracle!*

I slowly pushed my way up out of the crevasse with my arms, and sat there with my heart nearly pounding out of my chest. I peered down into the scary looking crevasse. *How did I keep from falling to the bottom?* I inched my way back from it, and slowly got to my feet. I looked back at my wife, "I'm okay!" I added, "Well this certainly isn't the proper way across." I then looked back at the other climbers. They had seen what had happened, and were now quickly roping up. "I think that's a great idea," I yelled back to them.

I moved back a few yards, then went around the end of the crevasse and soon was climbing above it. In a short time we were had covered the distance to the ridge, and off the crevasse field.

The rest of the climb was impressive, having some very exciting ice-climbing, and a lot of steep exposure, but it seemed secondary to the event that had occurred earlier. The summit of Mt. Hood was gained four or five hours later.

That evening after returning home, I opened the Bible, hoping to find some kind of answer to the miracle that had occurred on the mountain. I opened to the Psalms, written by King David. I knew that what had occurred this day was indeed a miracle, and it was confirmed in the verse I read. Psalm 91:11 & 12 states, "For he will command his angels concerning you, to guard you in all your ways; they will lift you up in their hands." *That must be the explanation!* There was no other reason that I could have survived in that manner.

As I thought about it, replaying it in my mind, I felt that the miracle had not only saved me, but also my wife's. The fall would have undoubtedly pulled my partner into the crevasse too. And then, what about the lives of the climbers following us? They had been un-roped until they saw me break through. If we hadn't been there first, would they have also gone into the same crevasse without being clipped to a rope?

This whole event had taught me a valuable lesson; I must take the time in the future to pray for my safety as well as the safety of others. *This was a lesson that would be used again.*

GENUINE DRAFT

Things are not always serious during climbs. If you have the right friends, you may experience many strange and funny experiences together. Since you don't have TV or other devices to keep you entertained, you have to look out for other sources to cheer up tired, worn out bodies. This story takes place in 1997.

Three of us, Gary Kepler, Mark Prince and I headed into the rugged Stuart Range to climb the west side of Mt. Stuart. It was early July and there happened to be a large snow pack that year at the higher altitudes. Our plan was to hike over Ingall's Pass, a four mile hike, with a steep and winding trail, then drop down into the basin, where we would follow Ingall's Creek another mile or two until we came to an area where we would camp overnight. Our climb would begin the next day.

The hike up to the top of the ridge was physically demanding. We took our break at the top of the ridge, and began viewing the terrain below us. We were surprised to find that the basin was completely covered in snow. It was a long break, eating the various goodies that we had brought with us for snacks, and re-hydrating our systems with water that we had lost sweating up the four mile hike. There, directly across from us was a beautiful view of Mt. Stuart. As we stared at our objective, I pointed out the West Ridge, a difficult climb that I had done with Steve Autio six years earlier.

"That was such a physical climb," I commented. "We headed out at the first light, camping down near the saddle adjoining the West Ridge. We didn't get back until late that night. Since we had to descend a different route, we chose the southwest ridge, a much easier descent, but one that placed us an extra mile or more away from our camp." I continued, "We were both so beat, without water for hours, and about ready to forget about getting back to camp that night. We made it back though, and boy were our butt's dragging. Back at camp, Steve had a big surprise for me. He had stowed away a couple of beers in a pile of snow near camp. He hadn't told me about hauling them up the previous day. He went over, dug them out, and we just sat there enjoying every drop. Nothing tastes as good as a cold beer when you are so thirsty."

"That's quite a story," replied Mark. "I wish we had thought of bringing in a few ourselves."

The snow was steep as we descended into the basin, and as we came closer to the bottom it began getting soft. Soon we were wading in knee-deep snow with our sixty pound packs. Not only that, but once we reached the creek at the bottom, we couldn't find an easy way across, as the water was high from the snow melt. We trudged along the bank, searching for a place to cross. Even worse, sections of the bank were covered with thick brush, and we were forced to push our way through.

Eventually, we found a crossing, but still managed to get our boots wet getting across. The nice wide path I had remembered when I had climbed in the area some years earlier was no place to be found, since it was still hidden by the snow and brush. On we plodded, becoming more tired and frustrated as we went. A hike that normally would have been only a little physically demanding had become a formidable obstacle.

Eventually, we came to an area that had patches of clearing beneath large trees, and this looked like a horse camp used by horse enthusiast's during the summer months. We dropped our packs and I told my companions to rest while I continued to walk up toward the mountain's flanks. I wanted to see if this area was close to where we would start climbing our route the following day. I soon came to a large gully that headed up steeply. I couldn't see all the way up the gully because it curved around a ridge, but I had a feeling that it probably was the route. I decided that we would camp below where we had dropped our packs and headed down to my weary climbing partners.

"This looks good to me," I exclaimed as I approached them. "Let's set up camp here. We also have plenty of water near here and won't have to pack it very far."

After taking a short break, I began setting up my tent while Gary and Mark decided to head down and get water for drinking and cooking their freeze-dried meals. In ten or fifteen minutes they returned with their water bottles and cooking pots full of water. After I had finished setting up my tent, I headed down for my water.

It was a muddy, wet path down to the creek that ran through bushes and small trees. I came to the end of the path and a spot that was obviously where hikers gathered their water. I stepped on a small rock a couple of feet out into the creek where the water was a little deeper. I took a water bottle, placed the end of the filter in it, and placed the other tube into the creek, beginning to pump the water into the bottle. I looked ahead at the swift running creek, wondering if this was the crossing for the horses in the summer. Glancing to my right something shiny caught my eye. About twelve feet away, where the swift water ran through some bushes was a shallow pool. In that shallow pool, bobbing up and down looked to be two beer cans. I finished filling the one bottle, then set it and the filter down on the bank. Being curious, I decided to get a closer look.

I moved along the bank a couple of yards, trying to get closer, without getting my feet wet. It looked to me like two black and gold colored beer cans in the water. I decided to get even closer, and carefully stepped on some small rocks in the creek. As I came closer, I reached down and picked up a small limb that had broken off from a bush. With the branch, and leaning as far as I could without falling in, I reached out and touched the cans, causing them to turn around. It was two beer cans. The lids were secure, and they seemed to be full. Was it possible that someone had actually left the beer there after taking them to the creek to cool them off? How long had they been there? It must have been late last summer before the fall and winter snow. Would the beer still be good, or would water have seeped into the can by now? There they were, two cans of Miller's Genuine Draft. I decided to leave them there for now. Possibly, after finishing the climb tomorrow, I would surprise my friends with them. I finished getting my water and headed back to camp.

The next day's climb was a rugged one. Mt. Stuart is the largest exposed chunk of granite in the United States. The mountain is steep, and none of the routes are very easy. The gully that I had chosen was very steep, with a mixture of soft scree, bushes, and boulders to climb over and around. I was hoping to get into a snow gully and follow it up, but we ended up on a long traverse over to the section of steep snow just below the false summit pyramid. We cramponed up the steep snow to the false summit, then from there scrambled on a very exposed ridge over to the main summit and to the top.

Coming down, I wanted to avoid going down the southwest ridge. It was the normal descent route since it was easier than other descent routes, but it would place us a long distance from our camp. I decided to head down the gully we had ascended earlier. I mistakenly got us off course a couple of times, and we had to do some steep scrambling to get back to our route. We were getting awfully tired, and were anxious to get back into camp as our throats were parched and burning from the lack of water. We had finished our water hours before. Thirteen hours after starting the climb we ventured back into camp.

We all immediately dropped our packs. Gary and Mark rushed down towards the creek, but I sat there and waited, hoping that they would not see the beer cans. Soon they returned, looking somewhat refreshed but continuing to drink down their water.

"Aren't you thirsty, they asked me?"

"I sure am. Did you leave any for me?" I joked as I grabbed my water filter bag and two bottles and headed down.

I was excited as I hiked down to the creek, hoping that the cans would still be there. I was hoping even more that the beer would not be stale or diluted. As I approached the place where I had first spotted them, I looked over to the little pool. I could not see them! The water had risen due to the heat that day and the snow melt. *Oh, No! They couldn't have washed away!* I stepped gingerly onto the small rocks and drew closer. Then I saw a shiny little gold and black can emerge from under the water. *They were still there!* I stepped into the water to get close enough to reach them, and then pulled them out of the pool. They seemed to be intact with no leakage. I quickly hid them in inside my parka, then finished getting my water. I headed back up with a smug grin on my face.

My friends had gathered some brush and were building a bonfire. It was starting to get a little chilly and the thought of a fire was very appealing. Once the fire was going, we just stood there, warming ourselves and watching it burn. There is something amazing about a nice fire in the wilderness. Of course, it was a good time to recall the day's events.

I couldn't hold myself back any longer and said to them, "Do you remember that story I told you earlier, about the beer that Steve Autio had hid, and pulled out of the snow bank after getting back to camp?" I asked.

"You bet!" came the reply.

"Well, I have some good news for you. How would you like to have some Miller's Genuine Draft right now?"

"Oh sure!" was Mark's reply.

Gary just replied with a **"Haw!"**

"I'm not kidding. I found two cans in the creek down there." They still looked at me like I was telling a dumb joke. Before they could respond, I reached into my parka pockets and pulled them out. "Check this out!"

The looks on their faces were priceless. They had really thought I was pulling their leg. What made it really special was that it had followed the story that I had told about Steve and his beers. Here we were, with two precious cans of beer in our midst. What are the odds of us finding anything like this at one little spot in the middle of the wilderness?

We still had to test the beer. We pulled out three cups from our eating utensils, deciding to divide the two beers three ways. We would have exactly eight ounces each, that is if the beer was still good. I carefully pulled the tab on one can. It foamed a bit, and that was a good sign.

"Metternich, you try it first. That way if it is bad.....", came their suggestion.

"You bet I will." I carefully poured what I thought was eight ounces into my cup. My friends watched intently as I lifted the cup to my lips, and tasted it. *Wow! It was good! So good!* "Hey guys, it's as fresh as the mountain snow."

We each sipped the beer like it was our last. Even though we were weary, our spirits were very high, not only from the success of reaching the summit, but from the little gift of gold and black cans that each of us shared.

At home, several days later, I thought, *I'm going to the store and get myself a six pack of that wonderful Miller's Genuine Draft, and really enjoy it.* After going to the store, I fixed some popcorn, poured my beer, and sat down to enjoy this precious liquid. To my utter disappointment, *it was blah!* That same beer, having the same flavor, but without the aesthetics of nature, the hard work, and excitement, was now just an ordinary beer.

EPILOGUE

The book only covers some of the special stories that are near to my heart. With over two hundred twenty summits of major mountains there are indeed many other stories and memories. Some good, and of course some bad. One thing that I have tried to balance over the years, is between being over confident (cocky), and being careful in my climbing. The feeling of invincibility seems to want to creep in, especially if you have not been involved in any major accidents. If you climb enough mountains, at some time in your career you will make mistakes, and there are times that unavoidable accidents just happen. Over the years, I was extremely fortunate that nothing really serious happened to me or to my climbing associates and students. And then, there is the "freak" accident that cannot be avoided.

After moving to Redmond, Oregon, I was getting back into good physical condition and looked forward to the hiking and climbing for the years to come. In was October 4, 2012, and I had just spent two nights camping on the shoulder of Middle Sister, a mountain of just over ten thousand feet. It had been a good climbing trip, although the weather dropped down into the twenties both nights. I had not seen any other hikers or climbers, probably due to the cold weather. I spent two nights at Arrow Lake, a beautiful spot nestled on top a rock buttress.

On the third morning, I put my sixty pound pack on and headed down the steep rocky trail. I reached easier ground and hiked along a beautiful stream, then back onto one of the main trails that would take me down the mountain.   My mind remembered the great times in this area in the years past, guiding climbing parties up North and Middle Sisters.

The trail was now steeper and with about three inches of dust accumulated from the summer. With my mind thinking about old times, I really wasn't concentrating on the trail. Suddenly, my feet slipped out from underneath me. With the heavy pack on my back, I went down fast and hard. As I fell, I pulled my left leg up to keep myself from sliding.

There followed a severe shot of pain from my knee that almost made me pass out. When I was able to regain my full focus, I realized that I had a bad injury in the knee area. I guessed I had torn my Quad Tendon, as in 2008 I had torn the tendon free from my knee cap on the right leg. It was the same horrific pain.   I took off the pack and tried standing up. The pain was less now, but if I moved the leg forward even a little, a jolting pain followed making me yell. No cellphone coverage, no people, and four and a half miles from the trailhead. I practiced walking with my hiking poles, attempting to not let the left knee go forward. I felt that I needed to try getting out to the trailhead on my own. I emptied my pack of everything I didn't think I would need, including my stove and tent. I kept the sleeping bag, a little bit of food, and little bit of water that I had left.

After hoisting the twenty some pound pack, I started down the trail. I moved slowly, letting the left hiking pole take over for the leg. It was horribly difficult, and when my knee went forward, every animal in the forest knew about it. I really didn't have much choice, as I knew my lady friend

Gale wouldn't even call the Sheriff's department until late that night. Besides, my pride hated the aspect of being rescued.

On I went, crossing a creek, stepping over logs, and the worse of it, having to down climb and scramble through an area of lava rock and boulders. I yelled out to God to help me. To keep my mind off the pain, I recited poems, sang songs, and even swore.

I thought that I had about a mile to go, and I was feeling confident that I would make it. I even praised the Lord for helping me to endure. Then, all of a sudden, I saw the parking lot! A rush of joy went through my whole body. Even though it would be difficult getting in the car and driving, I knew that I would make it home.

A week later I had surgery. As I suspected, the Quad Tendon was totally torn away from the knee cap and holes had to be drilled into my knee cap and the tendon tied onto it. My doctor, Blake Nonweiler did a great job, as also my physical therapist, Christy Mulloy. Nine months later I hiked up South Sister, a non-technical climb, yet twelve miles round trip with 5,000 ft. of elevation gain.

By that freak accident, I found out that I surely wasn't invincible. Because of the four and a half miles of being basically on one leg, it did some damage to my left hip, and I am still working at recovery.

I recently read the great Reinhold Messner's book, "Messner." In it, Messner, probably the finest high altitude climber in history tells about how a few years ago because his gate would not open to his manor, he had to climb the wall to get in. It was dark, and he slipped, breaking his ankle. His ankle still bothers him. Another freak accident.

GLOSSARY

BELAY   A method by which climbers
protect other climbers from falling. A rope is involved, that
attaches directly to the climber, and the other end to some sort
of anchor, or another climber.

BERGSCHRUND   A large crevasse located at the
upper most end of a glacier, separating the glacier from the
mountain itself.

BRECCIAS   Rock composed of angular
fragments of older rocks melded together. A poor rock to be
climbing on.

CARABINER   Sometimes referred to as
"biners," a small device made of light strong metal, oval in
shape having a gate that swings inward allowing the device to
be clipped onto a rope or other protection device.

CRAMPONS   Boot devices that fit underneath
the boot, made of light, strong metal, and having spikes that
can dig into ice or snow, giving the wearer secure footing.
Most crampons have front spikes that can be kicked into ice or
snow allowing the climber to climber steep terrain.

CREVASSE   A chasm on a glacier or snow
field of varying widths and depths formed by the river like
movements of the glacier downward. Crevasses can be from a
few feet to several hundred feet deep.

GORP   The hiker or climber's term for snack items to be eaten during an event. Gorp usually is made up of nuts and dried fruits.

HARNESS   A device worn by a climber with leg loops, and a waist belt made of strong material such as nylon. The climbing rope is attached to the harness, and in case of a fall, the climber will be stopped by sitting in his harness.

ICE AXE   An ice or snow climbing device, consisting of a shaft, with a pick and adze on one end. The adze is opposite of the pick, and is wide, allowing it to be used for digging or cutting of steps. Ice axes are normally made of light, strong metal.

ICE SCREW   A long tube, with screw like grooves, that can be screwed into steep ice or snow and can be used for protection against a fall by securing the climbing rope with a carabiner directly attached through the loop on the end, or using a nylon sling.

**LENTICULAR
CLOUD**   Sometimes referred to as cloud caps, the lenticular cloud is a very smooth, round or oval lensed-shaped cloud, which many times is seen hanging on the upper portion of a mountain. These clouds can be a fore warner of bad storms. If the cloud has settled on a mountain, inside them can have violent winds and freezing temperatures.

PENDULUM   A swinging movement made by a climber being attached to the end of the rope, with the upper portion of the rope attached to a safety device such as a bolt inserted into a rock face. By the climber running back and forth and gaining momentum, eventually the swing will take him to a desired location such as a platform, shelf, large crack in the rock, etc.

PINNACLE A part of a mountain that is towering, pointed, and usually rock, located on a ridge, or near the top of the mountain, or the summit itself.

RUNNERS Climbing devices, usually made of nylon webbing, either sewn circular, or with openings on each end for use in clipping a carabiner into some type of protection device such as a ring on a bolt, a cam device, ice screw, etc.

SCREE Very unstable loose dirt mixed with rock on a mountain slope, moraine, or on a steep hill.

SELF ARREST A physical maneuver involving the use of the ice axe to stop a fall, by laying and driving the pick, or adze into the ice or snow.

SNOW BRIDGE The un-melted ice or snow on top of a crevasse, which has not collapsed into the crevasse. The thickness can be from a couple of feet to yards thick. A person can be walking on a crevasse and not even knowing it, with a great hollow beneath him.

SPINDRIFT Very fine particles of snow or ice, like sand, that is blown by the wind in extremely cold conditions. The particles are fine enough to be driven through a water proof tent, and can pile up to several inches.

WEBBING A synthetic, nylon material made into a rope like device for use in attaching to protection devices, or used in slings.

PICTURES

MT HOOD- CREVASSE THAT I FELL INTO EARLIER THAT YEAR

THE STEEP WEST FACE OF MT. JEFFERSON WHERE WE BEGAN OUR DESCENT IN THE WHITE-OUT

BEGINNING OF WHITE-OUT ON MT. JEFFERSON CLIMB

A. MT JEFFERSON- LOOKING ACROSS THE RIDGE TO THE SUMMIT

B. ONE OF PINNACLES WE HAD TO CLIMB OVER

MT RAINIER- THE KAUTZ ICE CLIFFS IN CENTER OF PICTURE

THE ICE CLIFFS DIRECTLY IN CENTER OF PICTURE ON THE KAUTZ ROUTE, MT RAINIER

NIGHT ON RAINIER- 60 MPH WINDS

THE SUMMIT OF MT RAINIER IN A 60 MPH WIND AND WHITE-OUT

ROYAL ARCHES- ROTTEN LOG ROUTE

THE UNDERCLING AFTER THE PENDULUM ON ROYAL ARCHES

A WEARY BUT HAPPY GARY

A LOOK AT POPO FROM 17,442 FT IXTY

IXTACCIHUATL (IXTY) WITH POPOCATEPETL (POPO) IN
THE BACKGROUND. THE LIGHTNING STRUCK THE
HUT ON POPO AT 17,887 FT ALTITUTDE

BOB AND I AT HUT WHERE THE LIGHTNING HIT A FEW YEARS LATER.

THE SUMMIT HUT ON POPO WHERE THE LIGHTNING STRUCK
WHILE WE WERE INSIDE TWO YEARS LATER.

THE CASTLE ROUTE ON MT ADAMS

THE CASTLE HIGH ON A RIDGE ON
MT ADAMS. PHOTO TAKEN FROM THE AIR THE DAY PRIOR TO THE CLIMB.

C.E. RUSK'S ASHES ON MY KNEE ON TOP OF CASTLE

ON TOP OF THE CASTLE WITH THE ASHES OF C.E. RUSK ON MY KNEE.

THE AUTHOR AFTER MAJOR KNEE SURGERY SOLO CLIMBING THE WEST FACE OF MT SHASTA

MR CHARLIE BROWN
MY FAVORITE CLIMBING PARTNER

Made in the USA
Monee, IL
28 October 2021

80958873R00134